Discovering Tunisian Cuisine

Judith Dwan Hallet
Raoudha Guellali Ben Taarit
Hasna Trabelsi

Photography
Judith Dwan Hallet
Stanley Ira Hallet

Graphic Design
Stanley Ira Hallet

Table of Contents

Introduction

Soups

Salads

Briks

Tagines (Tunisian Style)

Couscous

Table of Contents

Meat

Stews

Fish

Desserts

Spices and Herbs

Courtyard, tomb of
Zaouia Sidi Ben Aissa,
Tebourba

Introduction

Judith Hallet on a rooftop
in the medina in Tunis

Judith Dwan Hallet

My first introduction to Tunisian cuisine was in 1964. I was a Peace Corps Volunteer teaching English as a foreign language (TEFL) to Tunisians at the Bourguiba School in Tunis. During my two-year stay, my talented and enthusiastic students often invited me to their homes for a traditional Sunday meal lasting the entire afternoon. It usually began with soup, followed by an unforgettable and unique appetizer called *brik à l'oeuf*, a deep-fried pastry filled with, among other things, tuna fish, capers, and an egg. After the *brik* they served us *Slata Tounsya*, a fresh tomato, cucumber, and pepper salad. Then there appeared the *pièce de résistance*, a traditional lamb couscous often accompanied with *harissa*, a hot spicy red pepper and garlic sauce. For dessert, they presented us with a large bowl of fresh fruit. The meal, or I should say feast, was not over. Our gracious hosts invited us to move to another room where they ceremoniously poured mint tea into small glasses garnished with pine nuts and served us with a seemingly never-ending array of sweet honey and almond pastries.

Conversation around the table often turned to their proud Tunisian heritage. The country has been at the crossroads of ancient civilizations, from the indigenous Berbers (the *Imazighen*) to the seafaring Phoenicians and the conquering Romans. After the fall of the Roman Empire, the Byzantines invaded Tunisia in the 6th century, followed by the Arabs 100 years later, then the Andalusians in the 15th century, the Ottomans in the 16th century, and finally the French in 1881. All of these cultures contributed to the extraordinarily diverse Tunisian cuisine that we enjoy today. For example, the origin of couscous dates back to the Berbers, while the honey pastries, like *Baklava*, appeared during the Ottoman rule in the late 16th century. As for the tomato and hot chili peppers, they became part of the Tunisian diet in the 19th century, via Spain, after the discovery of the New World.

Fifty years after my first visit, I was back in Tunisia. Khaldoun Ben Taarit, president and founder of l'Université Tunis Carthage, invited my husband, Stanley Hallet, Former Dean of The School of Architecture and Planning at The Catholic University of America, to transform the architectural design curriculum at his private university. Stanley and I had met fifty years earlier as Peace Corps Volunteers in Tunisia. After we finished our two years in the Peace Corps, we married, and the rest is history. Given such romantic ties to Tunisia, Stanley gladly accepted Khaldoun's invitation for both of us to return to Tunisia and for him to work with the university's architectural students and faculty.

During our month-long stay, Khaldoun and his wife, Raoudha, engaged Hasna Trabelsi, to prepare meals for us at our small boutique hotel, Dar Marsa Cubes, in La Marsa.

Stanley and Judith Hallet

Grand Mosque of Kairouan

Chenini

Grand Mosque of Kairouan

El Djem Coliseum

We sat down each night to a delectable feast that delighted all our senses. Hasna's meals were delicious, and her presentations were as colorful as the country's carpets, ceramic tiles, flowering plants, and the azure skies above the Mediterranean Sea.

Realizing that few people in the United States knew about this Tunisian Mediterranean diet based on the freshest of all possible ingredients, I wanted to try to prepare some recipes for my friends back in America. I looked for a good Tunisian cookbook online and in local bookstores. I found only a few cookbooks devoted to traditional Tunisian cuisine and even fewer written in English. When Khaldoun heard about my meager findings, he suggested that Raoudha, also an accomplished cook, and I write a cookbook together inspired by the family recipes passed down to Raoudha and Hasna by their mothers, mothers-in-law, and grandmothers.

With some trepidation, I accepted Khaldoun's offer. I had never written a cookbook, but then again, all my life I've been exposed to good food and I've always enjoyed cooking. My mother and grandmother were both excellent cooks. Every year, my family visited my grandparents for our summer vacation in Cannon Beach, Oregon. With the clams we dug up from the beach, my grandmother prepared homemade clam chowder. She also grilled Pacific coast salmon on the barbecue and served us fresh Dungeness crabs. The tastes of those meals still linger in my mind all these years later. My mother, Lois Dwan, was also an exceptional cook who liked to prepare a variety of dishes, be they American, French, Italian, Mexican, or Indian. In fact, she later became the acclaimed restaurant critic for the *Los Angeles Times*. During her reign from 1966 to 1984, she helped put Los Angeles restaurants and their chefs on the culinary map.

As for my own career, I didn't become a chef or a restaurant critic, but instead I became a documentary filmmaker. My interest in documenting other cultures around the world has continued over my filmmaking career and this curiosity and love of other cultures is a major reason why I agreed to collaborate with Raoudha and Hasna in writing a cookbook on the little-known but extraordinary Tunisian cuisine. It's my belief that through food, cultures can come closer together. What better way to break down barriers than by sitting around the table and eating a good meal.

In Tunisia, women are generally the cooks and reign in the kitchen. Raoudha and Hasna are no exception. They love to cook, and they took great pride in sharing their family recipes with me. In many ways, this cookbook is a personal journal recording my time with two fabulous women in their kitchens.

On the rooftops
in Tunis Medina

Judith Hallet
in the Roman town of Dougga

In the true spirit of passing their recipes on from one generation to the next, they introduced me to their cooking heritage and to their remarkable cuisine. Tunisia has many unusual and unique regional dishes. The recipes in this book represent Raoudha's own personal family recipes originating from the Tunis and Djerba regions of the country. The one exceptionl is Madfouna (Oxtail and Swiss Chard) that was Hasna's contribution. I picked the recipes that I most enjoyed. This book is by no means an exhaustive survey of Tunisian cuisine but rather an introduction to a culinary tradition that goes back thousands of years.

With my documentary film background, I wanted the cookbook to be a delight to the eye as well as the palate. For this reason, the photography and the graphic layout are important elements in the book. Stanley and I photographed the final dishes, which were prepared both in Tunisia and in the United States. It took us many hours and many tries to get the food and photography to look right. Once satisfied with the final photographs, Stanley, with his architectural eye, did the graphic layout for the book.

Writing down Raoudha's recipes turned out to be a complicated process. Hasna speaks only Tunisian Arabic. Since Hasna was the cook who prepared each recipe, each one of them had to be translated from Arabic to French to English. To do this, Raoudha, Hasna, and I sat around the dining room table, and Raoudha translated Hasna's Tunisian Arabic into French. I transcribed the French into English, hoping I got all the nuances. To more precisely measure the ingredients for our cookbook, I brought American measuring cups and spoons, asking Hasna to estimate by sight the measurements for each recipe. Given the challenges of translation and measuring in grams and kilos rather than ounces and pounds, the final measurements in this cookbook are only an estimated good-faith guide. Nevertheless, once back in the United States, I personally tested all the recipes and adjusted the ingredients to generally serve six people. I can't stress enough the importance of the creative process in cooking. Feel free to experiment and don't be afraid to add or eliminate a vegetable or a certain spice if you don't have it or if you don't like it. It's also important to adjust the amount of spices in each recipe to your personal taste buds. As for the hot, spicy Tunisian sauce, *harissa*, it is usually best to serve this as a side dish so your guests can decide to use it or not.

In the end, we hope this book is more than a cookbook, but also a visual journey into the world of Tunisia and her delectable food. So enjoy discovering this fine cuisine and as they say in Tunisian Arabic, *Sahha li-k* – To your health!

Hasna Trabelsi
with a lamb couscous

Raoudha Guellali Ben Taarit

Raoudha Ben Taarit and Judith Hallet

Raoudha and Khaldoun Ben Taaret, extended family and visiting American architectural studio critics

With this cookbook, I would like to take you on a journey to Tunisia, my beautiful small country that borders the Mediterranean Sea along the North African coastline. Its cuisine has a rich culinary heritage inspired by the many cultures and civilizations that have settled or passed through our country, going back, thousands of years. Today, Tunisian dishes reflect the input of all these cultures, making it a truly diverse, delicious, and healthful cuisine.

I decided to work with Judith on writing this cookbook when I discovered how overlooked my country's cuisine was by the rest of the world. Most people, including chefs, do not realize how closely tied the Tunisian cuisine is to the entire Mediterranean culinary experience. In fact, our Tunisian cuisine is one of the finest and most succulent examples of the Mediterranean diet, even cited by the Mayo Clinic as a "heart-healthy diet." Hopefully, with this cookbook, people will soon become as familiar with Tunisian dishes as they are with all our Mediterranean neighbors' cuisines.

Raoudha in the kitchen with her cook Hasna Trabelsi

The abundant use of healthful ingredients in the Mediterranean diet is mirrored in our diet in Tunisia.

Extra Virgin Olive Oil

Extra virgin olive oil is the major fat used in Tunisian cuisine.

Whole Grains

Whole grains like barley, bulgur, freekeh, and couscous are the main source of carbohydrates in Tunisian food.

Fresh Vegetables

Salads are made with fresh vegetables and are seasoned with extra virgin olive oil and lemon zest; they are generally served both at lunch and dinner.

Fish

Mediterranean fish is abundant off the coast of Tunisia, and many recipes have a variation that uses seafood.

Fresh Fruits

Fresh fruits are generally included in a Tunisian meal, usually for dessert.

Nuts

Almonds, pine nuts, walnuts or hazelnuts often accompany mint tea that we serve at the end of most meals and for afternoon tea.

While Tunisian cuisine is regional and based on our mothers' and mother-in-laws' recipes, my approach to Tunisian cooking is both classical and innovative. I fear that many ancestral skills and traditions related to the production and preparation of Tunisian dishes are quickly vanishing. For this reason, I've become an ardent advocate for the preservation of the oral history of Tunisian cooking that has traditionally been transmitted down from one generation to another.

Safeguarding Tunisian traditional cuisines, ingredients, and methods of preparation is not only about preserving part of my North African country's history and culture, it's also about telling the stories of the many people and civilizations that contributed to the development of Tunisia's food heritage.

This book is only a sample of the savory dishes we shared with Judith and her American friends. It's in no way a comprehensive collection of Tunisian recipes; rather, it's a selection of some of our most delicious and healthful food.

Typical blue door
in Sidi Bou Said

Jasmine flower vendor
in Sidi Bou Said

Khaldoun Ben Taaret and Raoudha invite Cindy Nguyen
and Stanley Hallet to a traditional couscous meal.

We also selected recipes that we felt were relatively easy to prepare and that contained ingredients available in the United States. The dishes come from different regions of Tunisia, depicting the richness of the diverse civilizations that influenced our country's culinary experiences. I invite you to join us on this journey, this adventure, to discover our Tunisian cuisine and its rich culinary culture. We are proud to introduce you to our own version of the Mediterranean cuisine, a feast for all senses.

Ingredients

- 10 sprigs fresh flat-leaf parsley, tied in a bundle
- 6 carrots, peeled and diced
- 3 leeks, white and light green parts, rinsed thoroughly, and finely chopped
- 3 stalks celery, finely chopped
- 2 zucchini, finely chopped
- 1 head kohlrabi, round root-like stem only, peeled and diced
- 1 medium yellow Yukon Gold potato, peeled, cut into small cubes
- 1 turnip, peeled and diced
- 1 clove garlic, peeled, minced or crushed with a garlic press
- 1 tablespoon ground turmeric
- 1 teaspoon ground coriander
- ½ teaspoon salt
- ¼ teaspoon freshly ground black pepper
- 1 tablespoon extra virgin olive oil

Note

You can use other fresh vegetables depending on the season. If you want, add a dab of *crème fraîche* to each serving bowl. Although not Tunisian but rather a French influence; Raoudha and I both agree—it's delicious.

Soups

Soup is a popular dish in Tunisia, especially during the winter months. Soup is often served as a first course or as the main dish for a light supper. During Ramadan, the Muslim month of dawn-to-dusk fasting, Tunisians like to break their daylong fast with soup. Turmeric, a spice frequently used in Tunisian cuisine and found in most Tunisian soups, is today often called the miracle spice, or the natural remedy of the century. Turmeric has many health benefits for treating arthritis, colitis, inflammation, dementia, diabetes, and the effects of aging.

Broudou
Vegetable Soup
Serves 8

This soup is made with fresh seasonal vegetables. It's often prepared when someone in the family isn't feeling well. Traditionally, Tunisians often added a chunk of bone marrow to this soup for its healing power. For more flavor, you can add ½ pound marrow bones, or a couple chicken legs to the stock.

Preparation

Place parsley, carrots, leeks, celery, zucchini, kohlrabi, potatoes, turnips, garlic, tumeric, coriander, salt, and pepper in a large pot. Add enough water to cover vegetables. Mix well, and bring to a boil over high heat. Reduce heat to medium-low, and simmer, covered, until tender, about ½ hour. Remove and discard parsley. Add olive oil to soup, and blend well. You can serve this soup leaving the vegetables diced or puréed in a blender.

Diced scallions

Chorba Frik
Freekeh Soup with Lamb
Serves 8

In spring, women from the countryside harvest the still-green barley to make this soup. They cook the barley, called *frik*, in a steamer, and then dry it in the sun. Finally, they take it to a miller for grinding. To earn some extra income, many women take ground *frik* to the market to sell, especially during the month of Ramadan when soup is one of the mainstays of *Iftar*, the evening meal that breaks the daylong fast. The closest grain to the Tunisian *frik* barley is freekeh, a whole grain wheat that is harvested while young and green. It's then roasted and cracked, leaving the internal grain with a nutty, slightly smoky flavor. If you can't find freekeh locally, you can order it online.

Freekeh

Ingredients

10 sprigs fresh flat-leaf parsley, plus more chopped for garnish
5 stalks celery: 2 whole with leaves, 3 diced
15 sprigs fresh cilantro
¼ cup extra virgin olive oil
5 scallions, white and light green parts, diced
½ teaspoon salt
¼ teaspoon freshly ground black pepper
½ pound boneless lamb, fat removed, cut into 1-inch chunks
2 tablespoons tomato paste
½ cup warm water
1 cup freekeh
½ tablespoon ground coriander
1 teaspoon ground turmeric
Lemon wedges

Preparation

Tie parsley sprigs, celery stalks with leaves, and cilantro together. Set aside. Heat oil over low heat in a large soup pot, and sauté scallions and diced celery until wilted, about 3 minutes. Salt and pepper lamb and add to celery and scallions. Lightly brown lamb on all sides. Dilute tomato paste with warm water, and add to the pot; mix well. Cover, and cook over low heat for 2 minutes, stirring occasionally. Add freekeh, coriander, turmeric, and 6 cups water. Mix well, and bring to a boil. As soon as water boils, reduce heat to medium, and simmer, covered, for 45 minutes. Add the tied bundle of parsley, cilantro, and celery. Cook another 10 minutes. Let soup sit for 5 minutes off the heat. Remove and discard parsley bundle. Taste, and add salt and pepper if necessary. Serve with chopped parsley sprinkled on top of each bowl of soup and lemon wedges on the side.

Note: You can substitute ½ pound boneless chicken breasts, or ½ pound flaky white fish for the lamb. If using fish, use 4 cloves garlic and ½ teaspoon ground cumin instead of scallions and coriander. Add fish during the final 10 minutes of cooking. Immediately remove fish from the pot. Remove and discard the bones. Cut fish into pieces and return to soup pot.

M'Hamsa
M'Hamsa Couscous Soup
Serves 8

This aromatic soup is scrumptious. *M'hamsa*, similar to Israeli couscous, is a hand-rolled sun-dried couscous with a toasty flavor. Vegetables, lentils, fava beans, chickpeas, and *m'hamsa* are the ingredients in this hearty soup. If you prefer the authentic *m'hamsa*, you can order it online or find it in Middle Eastern grocery stores.

Note

Chickpeas and fava beans need to be soaked in water overnight. If you don't have time to soak them, substitute canned chickpeas or frozen fava beans. Add to the soup at the same time as the *m'hamsa*.

Ingredients

3 scallions, white and green parts, diced
½ cup dried chickpeas, soaked in water overnight and drained, or 1 cup canned chickpeas, rinsed and drained
½ cup lentils, rinsed and drained
½ cup dried fava beans, soaked in water overnight and drained, or ½ cup frozen fava beans, rinsed and drained
2 carrots, peeled and diced
2 stalks celery, diced
½ head cabbage, cored, rinsed, and chopped into small pieces
2 tablespoons tomato paste
2 tablespoons extra virgin olive oil
2 tablespoons ground coriander
1 tablespoon ground turmeric
2 tablespoons paprika
½ teaspoon salt
¼ teaspoon freshly ground black pepper
½ pound fresh spinach, rinsed and finely chopped
3 fresh or 9 frozen artichoke hearts, thawed and halved
1 cup fresh or frozen sweet peas
1 cup *m'hamsa*, or Israeli couscous
2 tablespoons minced fresh flat-leaf parsley leaves, plus more for garnish
1 tablespoon minced fresh dill leaves, plus more for garnish

Preparation

In a large pot with 6 cups water, combine scallions, chickpeas, lentils, fava beans, carrots, celery, cabbage, tomato paste, olive oil, coriander, turmeric, paprika, salt, and pepper. Cover, and bring to a boil. Reduce heat to medium-low, and simmer for 35 minutes. Stir in spinach, artichoke hearts, peas, and cook 10 minutes longer. Add *m'hamsa*, parsley, and dill. Cook 15 minutes more, stirring once in a while. Taste, and add more salt and pepper if necessary. Serve with minced parsley and dill.

Note

Chickpeas and fava beans need to be soaked in water overnight. If you don't have time to soak them, substitute with canned chickpeas or frozen fava beans. Add to the soup at the same time as the barley.

Bourghoul
Bulgur Soup
Serves 8

This wholesome, healthful soup, which is tradiitionally made with bulgur, is easy to prepare. The bulgur in the United States is not the same as it is in Tunisia. Raoudha suggests you substitute pearl barley.

Barley

Lentils

Ingredients

1   cup pearl barley, rinsed and drained
½   cup dried chickpeas, soaked in water overnight and drained, or 1 cup canned chickpeas, rinsed and drained
½   cup lentils, rinsed and drained
½   cup dried fava beans, soaked in water overnight and drained, or ½ cup frozen fava beans, rinsed and drained
3   tablespoons tomato paste
1   tablespoon paprika, or 3 tablespoons if not using *harissa*
6   cloves garlic, peeled, minced or crushed with a garlic press
½   teaspoon salt
¼   teaspoon freshly ground black pepper
1½ tablespoons ground cumin
¼   cup extra virgin olive oil
2   tablespoons *Harissa* (p. 133), or store-bought, optional
2   lemons, quartered
    Lemon peel for garnish

Preparation

Put barley, chickpeas, lentils, and fava beans in a large soup pot with 8 cups water. Mix well, and bring to a boil. Skim off any scum floating to the top. Reduce heat to medium-low, and let simmer, covered, for 1½ hours, stirring every 15 minutes. Add more water if soup becomes too thick. Stir in tomato paste, paprika, garlic, salt, and pepper. Cook 15 minutes longer. Before serving, add cumin, olive oil, and *harissa* if you like it spicy. Squeeze lemon juice from a lemon wedge into each bowl of soup. To add color to this dish, garnish with tiny pieces of lemon peel. Although not in the Tunisian way, I like to also add chopped parsley.

Bulgur

Meatballs

Texture of dough

Hsou bel Kaâber

Soup with Meatballs   Serves 8

According to Raoudha, this is a marvelous comfort soup served during the winter months or when anyone comes down with a cold or the flu. It's made with the spicy sauce, *harissa*, and is served garnished with thinly cut lemon slices. To thicken the soup, Raoudha likes to add a flour and yeast batter to the soup. Tunisians love their *harissa*—but remember that it's spicy. If you wish a less spicy taste, you can leave it out and add more paprika.

Preparation

Mix flour, yeast, ¼ teaspoon salt, and warm water in a bowl. Cover with a dishtowel, and set aside at room temperature until the dough doubles in size, about two hours. See illustration. Place olive oil, tomato paste, *harissa* (if you like it spicy), paprika, 1 tablespoon coriander, turmeric, and garlic in a large pot with 4 cups water. Cover, and cook over medium heat for 20 minutes. Meanwhile, in a large bowl, mix together ground round, remaining 1 teaspoon coriander, 2 teaspoons mint, ¼ teaspoon salt, and pepper. Make 1-inch meatballs with the mixture. After the soup has cooked for 20 minutes, add the meatballs, and cook, covered, 10 minutes longer. Pour up to 1 cup water into the risen dough, stirring to make it a liquid batter. Pour the batter through a strainer and into the soup pot. Stir the batter well with all the other ingredients to prevent getting lumps. Cook, covered, for 7 minutes, or until the soup comes to a boil. Add remaining 1 teaspoon mint and capers. Serve in bowls garnished with fresh or preserved lemon slices on the side.

Straining dough mixture

Ingredients

½ cup all-purpose flour

2¼ teaspoons (1 envelope) active dry yeast
Salt

½ cup warm water

2 tablespoons extra virgin olive oil

1 tablespoon tomato paste

1 tablespoon *Harissa* (p.133), or store-bought, optional

2 tablespoons paprika, or 3 tablespoons if not using *harissa*

1 tablespoon plus 1 teaspoon ground coriander, divided

1 tablespoon ground turmeric

4 cloves garlic, peeled, minced or crushed with a garlic press

½ pound lean ground round

1 tablespoon dried mint, finely crushed, divided

¼ teaspoon freshly ground black pepper

1 tablespoon capers, drained
Fresh or Preserved Lemon slices (p. 135), for garnish

Salads

When I first lived in Tunisia as a Peace Corps Volunteer, each meal usually began with soup followed by a Tunisian salad made with ripe tomatoes, peppers, cucumbers, green onions, capers, and parsley. Garnished with olives and Tunisian canned tuna, it was heavenly. I've since learned that this salad is part of the Tunisian culinary heritage; in fact, healthful salads are an integral part of their cuisine. Most are easy to prepare, and all are nutritious.

The Vegetable Market
In La Goulette

Tunisians pride themselves on eating healthful meals replete with fresh fruit and vegetables. They grow their produce locally. Fruit and vegetable markets dot every neighborhood. Many farmers also sell their products from carts, pick-up trucks, and produce stands by the side of the road. Tunisian cuisine reflects the mainstays of the Mediterranean diet: fresh, well balanced, and healthful.

Tunisian Salad Dressing
Serves 6

The basic ingredients of a Tunisian salad dressing are always the same: extra virgin olive oil, freshly squeezed lemon juice, salt, and pepper. You can add Dijon mustard and garlic to this traditional sauce for most Tunisian salads.

Ingredients

Juice of ½ lemon
¼ teaspoon salt
¼ teaspoon freshly ground black pepper
4 to 5 tablespoons extra virgin olive oil

Preparation

Mix the lemon juice, salt, and pepper together. Slowly add olive oil, and mix well.

Variation: Mustard Dressing

Raoudha sometimes adds 1 tablespoon Dijon mustard and 1 garlic clove, minced or crushed with a garlic press, with the lemon juice, salt, and pepper.

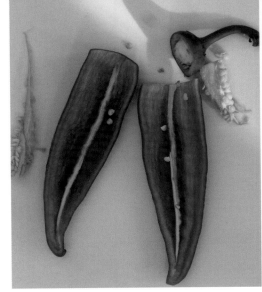

Pepper cut in half with seeds removed

Diced tomatoes

Diced
cucumbers

Slata Tounsya

Tunisian Salad   Serves 6

This Tunisian salad, made with finely chopped fresh vegetables and garnished with tuna fish, olives, and hard-boiled eggs, is light, bright, and beautiful. Raoudha likes to add a green apple for tartness. The cucumbers used in Tunisia are like the thin, small, Persian cucumbers. If you can't find them, substitute the long, thin English cucumbers. For a less spicy flavor, substitute ½ Cubanelle pepper for the Anaheim pepper, or for no kick at all, use ½ bell pepper.

Ingredients

- 4 tomatoes, cored and diced
- 1 Persian or ½ English cucumber, seeded and diced
- ½ Anaheim pepper, stems and seeds removed, diced
- 4 scallions, white and green parts, minced
- 3 tablespoons minced fresh flat-leaf parsley or mint leaves
- 2 teaspoons drained capers
- ½ lemon, cut into ½-inch julienne strips. or ¼ rind of preserved lemon (p. 135), minced
- 1 tart green apple, diced, optional Tunisian Salad Dressing (p. 25)
- ¼ (5-ounce) can tuna fish in olive oil, drained and flaked Whole black olives
- 2 hard-boiled eggs, quartered

Note

See chapter on Spices and Herbs to prepare preservd lemons, page 135.

Tunisians pride themselves on their canned tuna fish packed in extra virgin olive oil. You can buy Tunisian tuna fish and preserved lemons online.

Preparation

Place tomatoes, cucumbers, peppers, scallions, parsley, capers, lemons, and apples, if using, in a bowl. Pour on the Tunisian salad dressing and mix. Garnish with tuna fish, olives, and eggs.

Crushed peppers with mortar
and pestle

Ingredients

2 pounds Anaheim peppers,
    left whole
1 pound plum tomatoes,
    left whole
1 medium garlic head,
    left whole
1 teaspoon ground coriander
2 tablespoons extra virgin
    olive oil
½ teaspoon salt
¼ teasoon freshly ground
    black pepper

Peppers, tomato and garlic

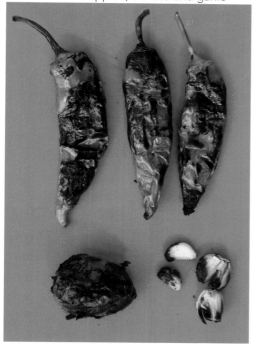

Slata Mechouïa
Grilled Vegetable Salad
Serves 6

Mechouïa salad is a typical dish often served as a first course or alongside grilled fish, lamb or chicken. It takes some time and practice to char the tomatoes and peppers, but it's worth the effort. Full of flavor, *Slata Mechouïa* is a popular dish among Tunisians. If you like a milder salad, replace the Anaheim peppers with Cubanelle peppers. Raoudha likes to add 1 small grilled eggplant to this salad even though it's not part of the traditional *Slata Mechouïa*.

Preparation

Char peppers on all sides on a grill, on a grill pan, on foil under the broiler, or by holding them with tongs over a gas range. Grill them over medium heat, using tongs to turn the vegetables, until the skins starts to blister and the peppers are charred enough to peel off the blackened skins. Let cool on a paper towel or in a clean paper bag for 15 minutes. Trapping the moist heat helps to loosen the skin. Use a small knife or your fingers to peel off the skins. Remove the stems, and cut the peppers in half lengthwise; remove all the seeds. Slice into long strips.

Char tomatoes over low heat using tongs to continually turn them over. Remove the blackened skin, and cut tomatoes in half. Use a strainer to drain the excess liquid. Char the garlic until soft. Use tongs to constantly turn them over. Separate the cloves from the head, discard the head, and remove the blackened skins of the cloves. See illustration.

Put all the cooled grilled vegetables on a cutting board and finely mince. Raoudha chops her vegetables using two knifes. See illustration. Place in a bowl and add the coriander, olive oil, salt, and pepper; mix well. Serve as a first course with some good bread, or as a side dish with grilled fish, meat, or chicken.

Blankit

Grilled Vegetable Canapés
Serves 6

For a zippy hors d'oeuvre, serve grilled vegetables, *Mechouïa*, on top of toasted slices of French baguette. If you don't like your food too spicy, use less *harissa*.

Ingredients

3 tablespoons extra virgin olive oil
1½ tablespoons white vinegar
1 teaspoon *Harissa* (p. 133),
   or store-bought, optional
1 French baguette, cut into ½-inch thick slices and toasted
2 cups *Mechouïa* (p. 29)

Preparation

In a bowl, mix olive oil, vinegar, *harissa*, and 1 tablespoon water. Dip each slice of toast into the olive oil mixture. Spread on a little *mechouïa*, and top with garnishes of your choice.

Suggested Garnishes
Pitted and diced black olives
1 (5-ounce) can tuna fish in olive oil,
   drained and flaked
Drained capers
1 finely-chopped hard-boiled egg
Grated Gruyère

Ingredients

2 pounds carrots, peeled
  and quartered crosswise
6 cloves garlic: 4 peeled and
  left whole, 2 peeled, minced or
  crushed in a garlic press
3 tablespoons extra virgin
  olive oil
1 tablespoon white vinegar
1 tablespoon *Harissa* (p. 133),
  or store-bought, optional
1 teaspoon ground coriander
1 teaspoon ground cumin
  Juice of ½ lemon
½ teaspoon salt
¼ teaspoon freshly ground
  black pepper

Suggested Garnishes

  Whole black olives, pitted
  Capers, drained
  Fresh flat-leaf parsley
  leaves, minced
2 hard-boiled eggs, quartered.
1 (5-ounce) can tuna fish in
  olive oil, drained and flaked

Slatet Omek Houria
Mother Houria's Salad
Serves 6

In Tunisian Arabic, "*Omek*" means "Your mother." Out of deference, Tunisian women of a certain age are called "*Omy*" rather than addressed by their first names.

I have always loved carrots. When Hasna first served this dish, I knew it had to be included in our cookbook. It's beautiful, colorful and simply delectable It's also easy to prepare. The Tunisian spicy sauce, *harissa*, gives this salad a zesty edge. If you don't like spicy, use less *harissa* or omit it.

Preparation

Steam carrots and 4 whole garlic cloves over boiling water until tender, about 25 minutes. Chop carrots and garlic into small pieces until well mixed. You can use a food processor, but keep it chunky. Transfer to a bowl. Add olive oil, vinegar, *harissa*, 2 minced or crushed garlic cloves, coriander, cumin, lemon juice, salt, and pepper. Top with garnishes of your choice.

Photo by Majib and Abdelwaheb Mahjoub

Fields of artichokes

Fields of grain

The Farm   *Les Moulins Mahjoub*

Abdelwaheb and Majib Mahjoub invited us to visit their farm, *Les Moulins Mahjoub* Estate, a one-hour drive into the countryside west of Tunis. Located near the town of Tebourba, the farm has been in the brothers' family for three generations. The Mahjoubs trace their Tunisian origins back to the Moors who were chased out of Andalusia in the 15th century. They settled on the lands of the ancient Roman town of Tiburbum Minus and the lands of the Berber tribe, *Oueslat*, who was famous for their cultivation of fruit trees. The Berbers and the Mahjoubs' Andalusian ancestors combined their agronomy and engineering talents to develop thriving agricultural farms around the town of Tebourba. Today the Mahjoubs have a 500-acre working farm and over 12,000 olive trees. Since the time of the Carthaginians (550 BC), Tunisia has been known for its olives, olive oil, and grains. With the Roman conquest of Carthage, Tunisia became the breadbasket of the Roman Empire.

Photo by Majib and Abdelwaheb Mahjoub

Photo by Majib and Abdelwaheb Mahjoub

Judith and Raoudha
in the artichoke fields

Fields of Artichokes

We visited *Les Moulins Mahjoub* farm during the month of May when the magnificent fields of artichoke plants were in full bloom. We couldn't resist walking through the rows and rows of shoulder-high plants, where we lost ourselves in a sea of green and purple.

Historically, artichokes originated as an edible food along the Mediterranean coast in Tunisia and Sicily. For over 2000 years, they have remained one of Tunisians' favorite vegetables, especially in spring when they are fresh, abundant, and inexpensive. We often heard the artichoke vendors roll their carts through the urban streets of Tunis calling out, "*ganaria, ganaria*", the Tunisian Arabic word for artichokes.

Tunisians use artichokes in many different recipes either cooked or raw.

Slatet Ganaria
Artichoke Hearts Salad
Serves 4

Slatet Ganaria is a delectable salad, but the artichokes must be extremely fresh if you want to prepare this dish the Tunisian way–raw. American artichokes need to be cooked for 20 minutes, otherwise the hearts will remain tough and quite bitter. Frozen artichoke hearts are an acceptable plan B.

Ingredients

4   fresh or thawed frozen
     artichoke hearts
1   thinly sliced
     lemon, halved
     Tunisian Salad Dressing or
     Mustard Dressing (p. 25)
     Finely chopped fresh flat-leaf
     parsley leaves for garnish

Preparation

If using fresh raw artichokes, remove leaves and choke, keeping only the hearts.

Squeeze some lemon juice on the hearts to prevent oxidation. Cook in a pot of boiling, salted water until tender, about 20 minutes. Do not overcook. Drain and let cool. Cut the artichoke hearts into thin slices.

Mix the salad dressing with the artichoke hearts. Garnish with parsley.

Slatet Brouklou
Cauliflower Salad
Serves 6

This salad is appealing to the eye and it goes well with other fresh vegetable salads or with a main dish such as grilled fish or meat.

Ingredients

1 cauliflower, cut into small florets
Tunisian Salad Dressing or
Mustard Dressing (p. 25)
Finely chopped fresh flat-leaf
parsley leaves for garnish

Preparation

Fill a medium-pot with water, and bring to a boil. As soon as it comes to a boil, add the cauliflower. Cook over medium heat for 4 minutes. Drain in a colander, and let cool. Transfer the cauliflower to a bowl. Add dressing, and toss to coat. Garnish with parsley. Serve at room temperature.

Chopped parsley

Parsley

Slatet Besbes

Raw Fennel Salad

Serves 6

When fennel is in season, enjoy this unusual salad. It's crunchy with a slight aftertaste of anise, and it's amazingly quick and easy to prepare.

Ingredients

1 fennel bulb, thinly sliced
¼ cup fresh minced flat-leaf parsley leaves
Tunisian Salad Dressing or Mustard Dressing (p. 25)

Fennel

Chopped Fennel

Preparation

Use only the bulb of the fennel. Remove the outer layer of the bulb if it looks too tough. Cut bulb into thin slices with a sharp knife or use a food processor with the slicing blade attachment. A food processsor is easier and faster than a knife. Transfer fennel to a bowl and add parsley. Add dressing to the fennel and parsley; toss to coat. Let sit for a few minutes before serving.

Slata M'fawra

Note

Green beans and/or diced fresh beets, make a nice addition to this salad. You should steam these vegetables separately. Instead of tossing the vegetables together, you can also arrange them alongside one another on one large serving platter as shown in the illustration.

Steamed Vegetable Salad
Serves 6

This lovely steamed vegetable dish is always a crowd pleaser. Not only is it healthful, but it's also colorful. If you can't find fresh peas, use frozen ones, and steam them only at the very end for 3 minutes. The peas need to stay *al dente*.

Ingredients

1 pound carrots,
  peeled and diced
½ pound Yukon Gold potatoes,
  peeled and diced
½ pound shelled fresh or
  frozen sweet peas
6 scallions, white and
  green parts, minced
2 tablespoons minced fresh
  flat-leaf parsley leaves
  Tunisian Salad Dressing or
  Mustard Dressing (p. 25)

Preparation

Steam carrots and potatoes for about 10 minutes, add peas, and cook until all vegetables are tender, about 5 minutes. Do not overcook. Drain vegetables, transfer to a bowl, and let cool. Add scallions and parsley, and mix well. Set aside to cool. Add dressing to the vegetables; mix well. Cover and refrigerate; serve cold.

Note

In season, it's nice to add other fresh vegetables such as asparagus. Cook the asparagus in boiling water for 5 minutes. Drain, plunge into ice water, drain again. Dice into small pieces, and add to salad. If you like a less spicy flavor, replace the Anaheim pepper with a Cubanelle pepper.

Ingredients

2 cups cooked white rice

Add as many of the following ingredients as you wish

3 tomatoes, cored and diced
1 Anaheim pepper, stems and seeds removed, diced
4 scallions, white and green parts, minced
½ Persian or English cucumber, seeded and diced
4 small cornichons or ¼ cup Oumelleh (p. 135), diced
1 tablespoon drained capers
¼ fresh or Preserved Lemon (p.135), with rind, diced
1 (5-ounce) can tuna fish in olive oil, drained and flaked (omit if used as a side dish)
Green or black pitted olives

Tunisian Salad Dressing or Mustard Dressing (p. 25)
1 hard-boiled egg, cut in wedges for garnish

Slatet Rouz

Rice Salad with Vegetables
Serves 6

This stunning multi-colored salad is delightful for a light lunch. You can also serve it as a side dish with grilled fish or grilled lamb chops. For the pickled vegetables, use canned or jarred giardiniera vegetables. If you prefer, make Oumelleh or Preserved Lemons, page 135. You can also buy pickled vegetables and preserved lemons online.

Preparation

Put the cooked rice in a serving bowl. Add your choices of the suggested ingredients and the dressing to the rice. Mix well. Prepare and add additional dressing if needed. Garnish with egg wedges.

Tunisian green peppers

Sliced and diced cucumbers

Ingredients to make the rice salad

Douiret, a Berber
mountain village
in Southern Tunisia

Hasna serving *briks*

Briks   A Traditional National Dish

Origins

No one knows for certain the origins of the Tunisian *brik*. There are three theories, however, that are well accepted:

Theory 1   The Berbers

The first theory traces the *brik* back to the indigenous Berber population, who have inhabited North Africa for over 7000 years. Since the *brik* also exists in Morocco and Algeria, many believe this Berber hypothesis makes the most sense.

Chenini, a Berber mountain village in Southern Tunisia

Village women in Douiret

Spice Bazaar, Istanbul

Briks

Theory 2   The Ottomans

The second theory suggests that the *brik* originated during the Ottoman Empire since its Turkish name, "*borek*," seems to be akin to the Tunisian word, "*brik*." The Turkish root of "*borek*," "*bur*," means to twist or fold.

Grand Bazaar, Istanbul

Süleymaniye Mosque, Istanbul

Briks

Theory 3   The Jews on the Island of Djerba

The third theory claims that the Djerbian Jews invented the *brik*. The island's Jewish population traces its roots back to the 6th century BC.

Tunisian Jews in their synagogue on the Island of Djetba

Note

Be sure to rinse and pat dry the parsley before you mince it.

Ingredient

1 small Yukon Gold potato
2 tablespoons minced fresh flat-leaf parsley leaves
1 tablespoon minced scallions, white and green parts
1 tablespoon drained capers,
1 (5-ounce) can tuna fish in olive oil, drained and flaked
¼ cup grated Gruyère,
2 tablespoons grated Parmesan, optional
½ teaspoon salt
¼ teaspoon freshly ground black pepper
½ teaspoon ground cinnamon
  Vegetable oil
4 *brik* pastry sheets (*malsouka*)
4 large eggs, as fresh as possible
1 lemon, quartered

Brik à l'Oeuf
Brik with Egg
Serves 4

This traditional dish is made with *malsouka*, a thin pastry dough similar to phyllo. It's generally served as an appetizer or first course. For the most part, Tunisians buy commercial sheets of *malsouka* at the supermarket. You can buy the *brik* pastry dough, *malsouka*, online or in Middle Eastern grocery stores. It's often called by its French name, *feuilles de brik*, or by its Moroccan name, *warka*.

During the month of Ramadan, the Muslim month of fast, *briks* are served practically every evening during *Iftar*, the evening meal that breaks the daylong fast. The best *malsouka* is prepared from scratch by Tunisian women using semolina, flour, water, and salt, something rarely done at home today. During Ramadan, however, it's a good source of income for women who can prepare the dough every day and sell it in the market places.

To eat a *brik,* pick it up with your hands and either bite into one end of the *brik* or directly into the middle of the *brik*. The goal is to eat it without the egg dripping onto the plate.

Preparation

Put the potato in a small pot of water, boil until tender, and drain. Peel the potato and mash in a bowl while still hot. Add parsley, scallions, capers, tuna fish, cheese, salt, pepper, and cinnamon; mix well and set aside.

Pour oil, ½-inch deep, in a large non-stick frying pan, and heat over medium-high heat. To test if hot enough, drop a small piece of *brik* dough into the oil. If it bubbles around the edges, the oil is ready to fry the *briks*.

While the oil is heating, fold the circular dough into a square. See illustration. Place potato mixture on the *brik* dough in the shape of a half moon, on one side. See illustration.

Crack the raw egg and place it in the middle next to the half moon filling. Quickly fold dough into a large triangle. Press edges to seal. Immediately put it in the frying pan.

Once in the pan, fry it quickly. Baste the *brik* with hot oil until it turns a golden brown. Turn it over and continue basting until golden brown. Don't overcook the yolk; it should remain like a soft-boiled egg. Remove with a slotted spoon, allowing excess oil to drain back into pan. Continue process with remaining briks. Don't worry if you don't succeed the first time. It takes practice. Serve immediately with quartered lemon wedges, which you squeeze over the *brik* right before you eat it.

Ground beef

Diced chicken

Note
Be sure to rinse and pat dry the parsley before you mince it.

Ingredients

Vegetable oil
½ pound raw medium shrimp, shelled, deveined, and finely chopped
2 tablespoons minced scallions, white and green parts
2 cloves garlic, peeled, minced or crushed with a garlic press
¼ cup minced, fresh flat-leaf parsley leaves,
4 brik pastry sheets (*malsouka*)
4 large eggs, as fresh as possible
1 lemon, quartered

Brik Variations

Ground Beef Brik
Serves 4

Make *Brik à l'Oeuf*, page 55, except substitute ¼ pound cooked lean ground round mixed with finely chopped scallions and minced flat-leaf parsley leaves for the tuna fish.

Chicken Brik
Serves 4

Make Brik à l'Oeuf , page 55, except substitute ¼ pound diced chicken sautéed in 1 tablespoon vegetable oil until cooked, about 4 minutes, for the tuna.

Shrimp Brik
Serves 4

Heat ¼ cup vegetable oil in a large frying pan over medium heat. Add shrimp, scallions, and garlic. Sauté until shrimp turns pink, 3 to 4 minutes. Don't overcook. Add parsley, and cook an additional 30 seconds. Remove from heat. Drain and discard excess oil, and transfer the mixture to a bowl. This is the filling for the brik pastry.

Pour oil, ½-inch deep, in a large non-stick frying pan, and heat over medium-high heat. To test if hot enough, drop a small piece of brik dough into the oil. If it bubbles around the edges, the oil is ready to fry the briks.

Fold the circular brik dough into a square. Place shrimp filling on the brik pastry dough in the shape of a half moon. See illustrations on page 55. Crack the raw egg, and place it in the middle of the brik pastry next to the half moon filling. Quickly fold the dough into a large triangle. Press edges to seal. Immediately put it in the frying pan with the hot oil.

Fry the brik, basting with the hot oil until it turns to a golden brown. Turn it over and continue basting until golden brown. Do not overcook the yolk; it should remain like a soft-boiled egg. Remove with a slotted spoon, allowing excess oil to drain back into pan. Continue process with remaining briks. Serve immediately with lemon wedges.

Swabâa Fatma

Fatma's Fingers
Serves 4

Fatma's Fingers are baked in the oven or fried in a pan. Raoudha prefers baking them. They are often served as an appetizer. You can buy the *brik* pastry dough, *malsouka,* online or in Middle Eastern grocery stores. It's often called by its French name, *feuilles de brik,* or its Moroccan name, *warka.*

This recipe works just as well with phyllo dough, easily found in most supermarkets. For a vegetarian dish, simply eliminate the chicken.

Fatma's Fingers

Note

Be sure to rinse and pat dry the parsley before you mince it.

Ingredients

Butter for greasing baking sheet
1 small Yukan Gold potato
3 tablespoons vegetable oil
1 medium boneless chicken breast
2 tablespoons minced fresh flat-leaf parsley leaves tablespoon minced
1 scallions, white and green parts
1 tablespoon drained capers
¼ cup grated Gruyère
½ teaspoon salt
¼ teaspoon freshly ground black pepper
½ teaspoon ground cinnamon
1 large egg
2 sheets *brik (malsouka)* or 2 sheets phyllo dough Melted butter to seal *briks*
1 lemon, quartered

Preparations

Preheat oven to 400°F. Grease a rimmed baking sheet with butter. Put potato in a small pot of water, boil until tender, and drain. Peel potato and mash in a bowl while still hot. Heat the oil in a large frying pan over medium heat. Add chicken and sauté until cooked through, about 7 minutes. Remove chicken from frying pan, and dice into small pieces. Place chicken in a large bowl, add potatoes, parsley, scallions, capers, cheese, salt, pepper, cinnamon, and egg; mix well. This mixture is the filling for the *brik.*

Cut the circular *brik* sheets in half with a knife or scissors. Put the filling along the straight edge of the dough. Fold the two sides to the middle, and then roll up the *brik.* It will look a bit like an egg roll. Brush it with some melted butter to seal. Put the *brik* rolls on the prepared baking sheet,– and bake until the *briks* turn a nice golden brown, about 20 minutes. Remove from oven and serve with lemon wedges.

Tagines
Tunisian Style

Tunisian tagine is different from its Moroccan namesake. It isn't cooked in a tagine terra-cotta bowl like in Morocco. Made with eggs, meat, cheese, and different vegetables, it's similar to an Italian frittata or a French quiche filling. Traditional Tunisian tagines are made with lamb, but you can replace the lamb with chicken or ground beef. Great for lunch or for a light supper served with a green salad and good bread.

Tagine Jben

Tagine Jben
Cheese Tagine with Lamb
Serves 6

This cheese tagine with lamb is the most popular and traditional of all the variations of the Tunisian tagines. You can substitute boneless chicken breast for the lamb. Tunisians always include meat in their tagines. Without meat, it's called *Maâkouda*, a marvelous dish for vegetarians.

Ingredients

Butter for greasing the baking dish
¼ cup extra virgin olive oil
½ pound boneless shoulder or leg of lamb
½ medium white onion, peeled and minced
½ teaspoon salt
¼ teaspoon freshly ground black pepper
2 teaspoons ground turmeric
1 tablespoon ground coriander
8 large eggs
2 cups shredded Gruyère or a mixture of Gruyère and Cheddar
¼ cup grated Parmesan
8 teaspoons cream cheese, in cubes, optional

Preparation

Preheat the oven to 400°F. Butter an 11-by-7-inch rectangular baking pan. Heat oil in a large frying pan over medium-low heat. Add lamb, onions, salt, and pepper, and sauté until meat is browned on both sides, about 2 to 3 minutes total. Add turmeric, coriander, and 2 cups water. Raise heat to medium, cook, turning meat occasionally, until most of the liquid has evaporated, about 18 to 20 minutes. Remove from heat. Dice lamb and return it to the frying pan. Lightly beat eggs in a large bowl. Add lamb, onions, shredded and grated cheeses, and if desired, cream cheese. Mix well. Pour into the prepared pan. Bake for 10 minutes at 400°F. Reduce temperature to 350°F. Cook until eggs are set, another 25 to 35 minutes. Serve with a green salad and good bread.

Tagine Sebnakh
Spinach Tagine with Lamb
Serves 6

Adding spinach to the traditional cheese tagine gives this dish extra color and taste. You may replace the lamb with boneless chicken breasts.

Ingredients

- 4 tablespoons butter plus more for greasing pan
- 1 clove garlic, peeled, minced or crushed with a garlic press
- 2 pounds fresh spinach, rinsed and not dried
- 3 tablespoons extra virgin olive oil
- ½ pound boneless shoulder or leg of lamb

- ½ medium white onion, peeled and minced
- ½ teaspoon salt
- ¼ teaspoon freshly ground black pepper
- 2 teaspoons ground turmeric
- 1 tablespoon ground coriander
- 8 large eggs
- 1 cup grated Gruyère or Cheddar, or mixture of both
- 3 tablespoons grated Parmesan
- 8 teaspoons cream cheese in cubes, optional

Preparation

Preheat oven to 400°F. Butter an 11-by-7-inch rectangular baking dish. Heat 4 tablespoons butter in a large frying pan over medium heat. Add garlic, and sauté for 30 seconds to release aroma. Be careful not to burn. Add spinach, and sauté until wilted, about 2 minutes. Drain and finely chop spinach yielding approximately 2 cups chopped spinach. Set aside. Add oil to frying pan and heat over medium heat. Add lamb, onions, salt, and pepper and sauté for 2 to 3 minutes, or until meat is browned on both sides.

Add turmeric, coriander, and 2 cups water. Continue to cook over medium heat, turning meat occasionally, until most of the liquid has evaporated, about 30 minutes. Remove from heat. Dice lamb and return it to the frying pan with cooked onions. Lightly beat eggs in a large bowl. Add diced meat, onions, spinach, cheeses, and if desired, cream cheese. Blend well. Pour into the greased pan. Bake for 10 minutes at 400°F. Reduce temperature to 350°F. Cook until eggs are set, another 25 to 35 minutes.

To test when ready, insert a thin-bladed knife into the center of the tagine. It should come out clean. Serve with a green salad and good bread.

Tagine Variations

Parsley, Sweet Pea, Potato, Ricotta, and Feta Tagines
Serves 6

There are many different versions of tagines. You can replace the spinach in the Spinach Tagine with Lamb, page 63, with any one of the ingredients mentioned below. Each variation on the theme has its own proper name.

Tagine *Mâadnouss*: 2 cups minced flat-leaf parsley leaves
Tagine *Jelbana*: 2 cups fresh or frozen sweet peas
Tagine *Batata*: 2 cups cooked, peeled and diced Yukon Gold potatoes
Tagine *Ricotta*: 1 cup ricotta, well drained
Tagine *Feta*: 1 cup feta, well drained

You can also mix two different ingredients together, like potatoes with parsley, or spinach with peas. You can also add 2 cups chopped grilled peppers, zucchini, or eggplant. There is no limit to the variations for this popular Tunisian dish. Have fun. Experiment.

Tagine Malsouka
Brik Tagine
Serves 6

This method can be used for any of the tagines in this cookbook.

Lay sheets of *brik* (*malsouka*) in a greased 8-inch baking pan. Place tagine mixture of your choice on top of the *brik* sheets. Fold over the sheets to cover the Tagine. If you don't have sheets of *brik* dough, use phyllo dough.

I had two sheets of *brik* dough left over, so I wrapped a tagine in the sheets of *brik* in a 5-inch round cooking mold. This free form tagine looked spectacular and it was a big hit when I served it to my guests. With Tunisian cuisine, it's always fun to use your imagination to create something different.

Tunisian
sun-dried
couscous

Couscous
History

Couscous is an iconic dish in Tunisia, as it is in all North African countries. It dates back at least 3000 years to the indigenous population of North Africa, the Berbers. Each country, even each region, has its own style of couscous. Tunisians prefer using a finer grain than their Moroccan and Algerian neighbors.

Tunisians generally serve their couscous with lamb, but it's also often served with chicken, fish, or simply vegetables. Every region in Tunisia prides itself on its own unique preparation of couscous. The couscous dishes in this cookbook are Hasna's and Raoudha's favorite family recipes passed down to them over the generations.

The traditional way to prepare the couscous grains involves a *couscousière*, a special kind of steamer. Steaming the couscous imbues the grains with the flavors from the meat and spices cooking in the lower part of the *couscousière*. If possible, buy the loose couscous sold in bins in upscale grocery stores or health food stores. If you can't find the loose couscous, buy the commercial packaged couscous, and follow the directions on the box.

If you have a *couscousière* or steamer, you can cook the couscous over the stock in the top part of the *couscousière* or steamer. If using commercial packaged couscous, Raoudha suggests adding 1 teaspoon cinnamon to the grains while they are cooking.

Hasna serves a lamb and vegetable couscous

Icha, Zazia, Bornia
and Gzala sift the
wheat from the chaff.

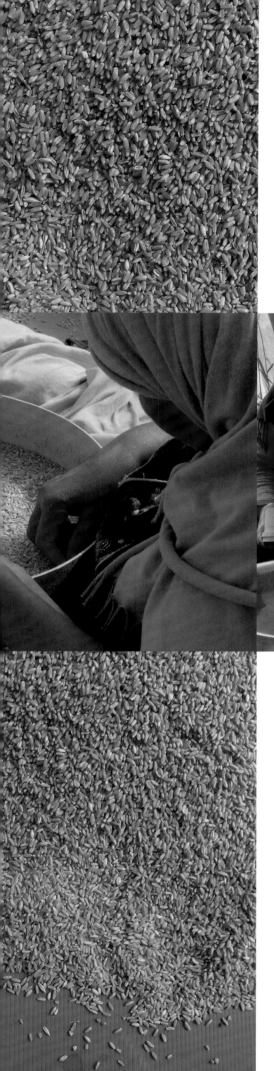

Women from the countryside seperate the wheat from the chaff in the ancient traditional Berber way.

Couscous is formed from a type of North African semolina made from crushed durum wheat. To make couscous grains in the traditional way, women sprinkle the wheat with water and hand roll it to form small grains of couscous. They sift the grains through a sieve and then dry them in the sun.

Making couscous by hand is a tradition passed down from mother to daughter or daughter-in-law. Raoudha and Hasna insist that this handmade sun-dried method makes the very best couscous. In the past, groups of women came together to make large batches of couscous grains over several days. Sadly, this tradition is rapidly falling out of favor, because it's too labor intensive. Couscous production today is largely mechanized for distribution in markets around the world.

Note

Chickpeas need to be soaked in water overnight. If you don't have time to soak them, use canned chickpeas.

Tunisians often serve fermented milk as an accompanying drink; in the United States, you can use buttermilk.

Ingredients

2   cups couscous

2   tablespoons extra virgin olive oil

2½ pounds bone-in shoulder or leg of lamb, or 1½ pounds boneless, cut in 6 pieces

½   cup dried chickpeas, soaked in water overnight and drained, or 1 cup canned

1   medium white onion, peeled and thinly sliced

½   cup extra virgin olive oil

2   tablespoons tomato paste

1   tablespoon paprika

1   teaspoon ground turmeric

1   tablespoon ground coriander

1   teaspoon salt

¼   teaspoon freshly ground black pepper

2   cups couscous

½   pound butternut squash, peeled, seeded, and sliced lengthwise

2   Anaheim or Poblano peppers, stems and seeds removed, quartered

Couscous Allouche
Lamb Couscous
Serves 6

Raoudha uses the bone-in shoulder or leg of lamb which she has cut by the butcher. She says the bones boost the flavor. It's also just as hearty with the boneless lamb. Today many Tunisians substitute 1½ pounds bone-in chicken breast or thighs for the lamb.

Tunisians use a fairly hot chili pepper in their couscous but I prefer the milder Anaheim or Poblano pepper. If you like it even less spicy, use 1 Cubanelle pepper instead.

Preparation

Pour couscous grains in a bowl. Add ¼ cup water, a few drops at a time, mixing well with your hands so that all the grains are evenly moistened. Add olive oil, and mix well with your hands. If using packaged couscous, you don't need a steamer; just follow directions on the box.

Place lamb, chickpeas, onions, olive oil, tomato paste, paprika, turmeric, coriander, salt, and pepper in a large bowl. Mix all together, making sure the spices blend well with the lamb.

Place lamb mixture in the bottom part of a *couscousière*. Cover the lamb mixture with 6 cups water. Bring to a boil. Put the couscous in the top part of the *couscousière*. The aromas from the stock need to permeate the couscous. The moment you see the steam rising through the couscous grains, cook for 30 more minutes over medium heat. Add squash and peppers to stock. Cook 15 more minutes.

Place couscous on a large platter. Break up any lumps before serving. Pour two ladles of stock over couscous and mix well, ensuring that couscous grains are evenly moistened. If needed, add more stock until grains can no longer absorb the stock. Garnish couscous platter with squash, peppers and lamb. Serve remaining stock on the side.

Couscous Allouche bel Khodhra

Lamb Couscous with Vegetables
Serves 6

Couscous Allouche bel Khodhra is made with a variety of fresh vegetables and can be made vegetarian by eliminating the meat. You can also substitute 1½ pounds bone-in chicken breast or thighs for the lamb.

Note

The chickpeas need to be soaked overnight. If you don't have time to soak them, use canned chickpeas.

Ingredients

2   cups couscous
2   tablespoons extra virgin olive oil
2½ pounds bone-in shoulder or leg of lamb, or 1½ pounds boneless, cut in 6 pieces
½   cup dried chickpeas, soaked in water overnight and drained, or 1 cup canned chickpeas, rinsed and drained
1   medium white onion, peeled and thinly sliced
½   cup extra virgin olive oil
2   tablespoons tomato paste
1   tablespoon paprika
1   teaspoon ground turmeric
1   tablespoon ground coriander
1   teaspoon salt
¼   teaspoon freshly ground black pepper
½   pound butternut squash, peeled, seeded, and sliced lengthwise
2   Anaheim peppers, stems and seeds removed, quartered

Suggested Vegetables

2   carrots, peeled and halved lengthwise
2   small potatoes, peeled and halved
1   zucchini, quartered
1   turnip, peeled and quartered
½   cabbage, cored and quartered
1   bundle Swiss chard, ribs removed, chopped
4   whole scallions
¼   pound green beans, stems removed
½   pound asparagus

Preparation

Pour couscous grains in a bowl. Add ¼ cup water, a few drops at a time, mixing well with your hands so that all grains are evenly moistened. Add olive oil, and mix well with your hands. If using packaged couscous, you don't need a steamer; just follow directions on the box.

Place lamb, chickpeas, onions, olive oil, tomato paste, paprika, turmeric, coriander, salt, and pepper in a large bowl. Mix all together, making sure the spices blend well with the lamb. Place lamb mixture in the bottom part of a *couscousière*. Cover with 6 cups water. Bring to a boil. Put the couscous in the top part of the *couscousière*. The aromas from the stock need to permeate the couscous. The moment you see the steam rising through the couscous grains, cook for 30 more minutes over medium heat. Add squash, peppers and vegetables of your choice to the stock. Cook until vegetables are tender, 15 minutes more. Remove all vegetables from stock.

Place couscous on a large deep platter. Break up any lumps before serving. Pour two ladles of stock over couscous and mix well, ensuring that couscous grains are evenly moistened. If needed, add more stock until grains can no longer absorb the stock. Garnish couscous with vegetables and meat. Serve remaining stock on the side.

Couscous bel Hout
Fish Couscous   Serves 6

For the fish, buy a whole red snapper or grouper. Have fish monger save the fish head for the stock.

Ingredients

2   cups couscous
2   tablespoons extra virgin olive oil
2   tablespoons tomato paste
5½ cups boiling water, divided
6   tablespoons olive oil, divided
5   cloves garlic, peeled, minced or crushed with a garlic press
1   medium white onion, peeled and thinly sliced
1   tablespoon ground cumin
1   tablespoon paprika
½   cup dried chickpeas, soaked in water overnight and drained, or 1 cup canned chickpeas, rinsed and drained
1   tablespoon ground turmeric
1   teaspoon salt
¼   teaspoon freshly ground black pepper
½   pound butternut squash, peeled, seeded, and sliced lengthwise
2   Anaheim peppers, stems and seeds removed, quartered
3   pounds whole red snapper or grouper, scaled, cleaned, cut into 6 pieces
1   fish head from cut-up whole fish

Note

Chickpeas need to be soaked overnight. If you don't have time to soak them, use canned chickpeas.

Preparation

Pour couscous grains in a bowl. Add ¼ cup water, a few drops at a time, mixing well with your hands so that all the grains are evenly moistened. Add 2 tablespoons olive oil, and mix well with your hands. If using packaged couscous, you don't need a steamer; just follow directions on the box. Dilute tomato paste in ½ cup boiling water. Set aside. Pour olive oil into the bottom part of the *couscousière*. Set over low heat. Add garlic. Sauté approximately 30 seconds. Add onions. Sauté 20 more seconds. Add cumin. Sauté 10 more seconds. Add paprika and diluted tomato paste. Bring to a boil, and cook for 3 to 4 minutes to rid tomato paste of its bitter acidic taste. Add chickpeas, turmeric, salt, pepper, and remaining 5 cups boiling water in bottom part of a *couscousière*.

Put couscous grains in top part of *couscousière*. When you see the steam rising through the couscous grains, cook for 30 more minutes over medium heat. Add squash, peppers, and fish head to stock in bottom part of pot. Cook 5 more minutes. Remove and discard fish head. Add fish to stock and cook 10 more minutes. Place couscous on a serving dish. Break up any lumps before serving. Pour two ladles of stock over couscous and mix well, ensuring that couscous grains are evenly moistened. If needed, add more stock until grains can no longer absorb stock. Place fish, squash, peppers, and chickpeas over couscous.

Ingredients for Fish

5 cloves garlic, peeled, minced or crushed with a garlic press
1 cup diced scallions, white and green parts
1 tablespoon ground cumin
2 tablespoons minced fresh dill leaves
1 tablespoon ground turmeric
1 tablespoon paprika
1 teaspoon salt
¼ teaspoon freshly ground black pepper
3 pounds whole red snapper or grouper, scaled, cleaned, cut into 6 pieces
3 cups minced fresh flat-leaf parsley leaves
3 cups fresh spinach, finely chopped
1 tablespoon tomato paste
¼ cup extra virgin olive oil
2 medium Yukon Gold potatoes, peeled and quartered
2 carrots, peeled and halved

Ingredients for Fish Stock

2 tablespoons tomato paste
½ cup boiling water
6 tablespoons olive oil, divided
5 cloves garlic, peeled, minced or crushed with a garlic press
1 medium white onion, peeled and thinly sliced
1 tablespoon ground cumin
1 tablespoon paprika
1 tablespoon ground turmeric
1 teaspoon salt
¼ teaspoon freshly ground black pepper
6 cups boiling water
2 cups couscous
2 tablespoons extra virgin olive oil
½ small butternut squash, peeled, seeded, cut into 6 slices
3 Anaheim or Cubanelle peppers, left whole
1 fish head, from cut-up whole fish, optional

Couscous Djerbi bel Hout

Djerbian-Style Fish Couscous
Serves 6

Couscous Djerbi bel Hout originated on the island of Djerba. This traditional recipe has been passed down through Raoudha's father's side of the family which is of Berber descent and has lived in Djerba for thousands of years.

Preparation of Fish

In a bowl, mix together garlic, scallions, cumin, dill, turmeric, paprika, salt, pepper, and spread all over fish, seasoning it well. Mix parsley, spinach, tomato paste, and olive oil in a bowl. Spread over fish to cover. Add potatoes and carrots. Set aside.

Preparation of Fish Stock

Dilute tomato paste in ½ cup boiling water. Set aside. Pour olive oil into the bottom part of the *couscousière*. Set over low heat. Add garlic. Sauté approximately 30 seconds. Add onions. Sauté 20 more seconds. Add cumin. Sauté 10 more seconds. Add paprika and diluted tomato paste. Bring to a boil, and cook for 3 to 4 minutes to rid tomato paste of its bitter acidic taste. Add turmeric, salt, pepper, and boiling water in bottom part of the *couscousière*. Place marinated fish pieces with the spinach, potatoes and carrots in top part of the *couscousière*, and let steam over the stock for 30 minutes over medium heat.

Meanwhile, pour couscous grains in a bowl. Add ¼ cup water, a few drops at a time, mixing well with your hands so that all grains are evenly moistened. Add olive oil, and mix well with your hands. Bring water to boil in the lower part of a separate steamer. If using packaged couscous, just follow directions on the box. Put couscous in the top part of the steamer over the boiling water. The moment steam begins to penetrate the couscous grains, cook for 30 more minutes over medium heat.

After fish stock has cooked for 30 minutes, add squash, peppers, and optional fish head to stock. Cook 10 more minutes. Remove and discard fish head. Remove squash and peppers and set aside on a cutting board. Quarter and seed peppers. Place cooked couscous on a large, deep platter. Break up any lumps before serving. Pour two ladles of stock over couscous and mix well, ensuring that couscous grains are evenly moistened. If needed, add more stock until grains can no longer absorb stock. Remove fish and spinach from the *couscousière*. Garnish couscous with fish, squash, and peppers. You can also garnish with peppers, grilled separately, as illustrated. Serve remaining stock in a separate bowl.

Couscous el Farah
Wedding Couscous
Serves 6

Wedding celebrations are a big deal in Tunisia, sometimes lasting three days. It's a custom to serve this special bridal couscous on the night before the wedding ceremony. Please note the chickpeas need to be soaked overnight. If you don't have time to soak them overnight, use canned chickpeas.

Orange blossom water
and lamb for wedding coucous

Ingredients

- 2 cups couscous
- 2 tablespoons extra virgin olive oil
- 2½ pounds bone-in shoulder or leg of lamb, or 1½ pounds boneless, cut in 6 pieces
- 6 scallions, white and light green parts, diced
- ½ cup dried chickpeas, soaked in water overnight and drained, or 1 cup canned chickpeas, rinsed and drained
- ½ cup extra virgin olive oil
- 2 tablespoons tomato paste
- 1 tablespoon paprika
- 1 tablespoon ground turmeric
- ½ cup raisins
- ½ cup orange blossom water
- 1 teaspoon ground cinnamon
- ½ small butternut squash, peeled, seeded, and quartered, optional
- 2 Anaheim peppers, left whole, optional
- 1 zucchini, quartered, optional

Preparation

Pour couscous grains in a bowl. Add ¼ cup water, a few drops at a time, mixing well with your hands so that all grains are evenly moistened. Add 2 tablespoons of olive oil, and mix well with your hands. If using packaged couscous, you don't need a steamer; just follow directions on the box.

In a large bowl, mix lamb with scallions, chickpeas, ½ cup olive oil, tomato paste, paprika, and turmeric. Let marinate for at least 30 minutes. You can prepare this the day before and marinate, cover, overnight in the refrigerator. Soak raisins in orange blossom water in a medium bowl for 20 minutes.

Put lamb and its marinade in bottom of a *couscousière*, and add 6 cups water. Cover and bring to a boil over medium heat. Add couscous grains to top part of *couscousière*. The aromas from the stock need to permeate the couscous. The moment you see the steam rising through the couscous grains, cook for 30 more minutes over medium heat. Add one ladle of stock to raisins in orange blossom water. Set aside. Stir cinnamon, butternut squash, peppers, and zucchini into stock in bottom part of *couscousière*. Continue cooking for 15 more minutes. Drain the raisins and add liquid to stock. Put couscous on a large platter. Break up any lumps before serving. Pour two ladles of stock over couscous and mix well, ensuring that couscous grains are evenly moistened. If needed, add more stock until grains can no longer absorb stock. Garnish with lamb, chickpeas, vegetables, and raisins.

Nadhir and Abelwahed Mansouri

Meat
The Butcher Shop

Most Tunisians buy their meat at a butcher shop where they can personally specify the quality and size of the cuts of meat. They prefer their meat freshly slaughtered. If an animal's head is hanging in the shop's window, people know it has been slaughtered and cut up that day. Raoudha's favorite butcher, Abdelwahed Mansouri, has his own shop in Ariana, a suburb of Tunis. She has been purchasing her meat and *merguez* sausages from Abdelwahed for over 18 years. Now his son, Nadhir, has taken over the role as chief butcher.

Lamb is the most popular meat in Tunisian cuisine, especially to make with couscous. Lamb chops, lamb liver, and *merguez* sausages, grilled on a charcoal wood barbecue are also favorites.

Since Tunisia is an Islamic country, most Tunisians don't eat pork, because it's forbidden in the *Sharia*, Islamic religious law. In fact, butchers must follow the *Halal* practice on how to slaughter and prepare their meat as prescribed by *Sharia* law.

Côtelettes Mechouïa
Grilled Lamb Chops
Serves 6

Tunisians often prepare their lamb chops and *merguez* sausages together on the grill, as illustrated. When cooked on a barbecue over a layer of rosemary and thyme sprigs in the Tunisian manner, the meat absorbs the flavor and aroma of the fresh herbs. It's simply divine.

Merguez sausages

Ingredients

1 teaspoon salt
6 lamb chops
  Sprigs of rosemary or thyme, or both

Preparation

Salt the lamb chops. Rub rosemary or thyme sprigs on the chops. Place the sprigs on the grill. Place lamb chops on the herbs. The aroma from the herbs will penetrate the lamb, giving it a lovely flavor. Grill 4 to 5 minutes on each side, depending on how well done you like your chops.

Grilled Lamb Chops
in America

In the United States, lamb chops are thicker than those in Tunisia, but the result is the same. Just to be sure this method of barbecuing meat would work at home, I tried grilling thick American lamb chops on our typical backyard barbecue. The results were just as extraordinary: succulent, aromatic, and memorable.

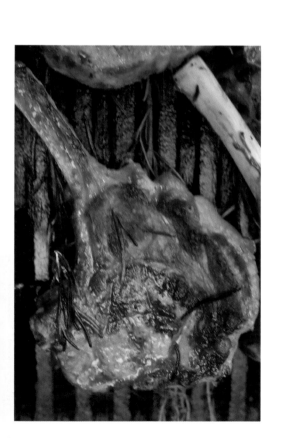

Madfouna
with
couscous

Swiss chard

Madfouna
Oxtail Stew with Swiss Chard
Serves 6

Madfouna is also a traditional Tunisian Jewish dish served on the Sabbath. Tunisian Jews call it *P'kayla*. It's a special dish that our friend and retired restaurant chef, Moncef Meddeb, insisted we include in our cookbook. According to Moncef, it's one of the grand dishes of Tunisian cuisine, although he describes it as looking like the debris dredged up from the bottom of a pond, dark and muddy. This stew was well worth the effort and certainly one of the most delicious meat dishes we had in Tunisia. Hasna says to allow 4 hours for prep and cooking time.

Ingredients for Stew

	Extra virgin olive oil
4	pounds Swiss chard leaves, stems removed
12	cloves garlic, peeled and minced
8	scallions, white and light green parts, finely diced
2	tablespoons paprika
2	tablespoons ground coriander
1	teaspoon salt
¼	teaspoon freshly ground black pepper
2	pounds oxtail, fat removed, cut into 2 to 2½-inch pieces
1	cup canned white beans, rinsed and drained

Ingredients for Meatballs

½	pound lean ground beef
1	teaspoon coriander
1	tablespoon dried mint leaves, finely crushed
2	cloves garlic, peeled, minced or crushed with a garlic press
½	teaspoon salt
¼	teaspoon freshly ground black pepper

Preparation

Pour enough olive oil to cover the bottom of two large frying pans, and heat the oil over low heat. Divide the Swiss chard into 4 portions. Add 1 portion to each pan. Sauté the chard stirring constantly, until the chard turns dark. Be careful not to burn the chard. Transfer the chard from the frying pans to a large bowl. Repeat the process with the remaining Swiss chard. Transfer all the cooked chard to a cutting board. and finely chop with a knife.

Cover the bottom of a large pot with a thin layer of olive oil; heat oil over medium-low heat. Add garlic, scallions, paprika, coriander, salt, and pepper. Add oxtail, and brown the meat on all sides to seal in its flavors. In another pot, boil 5 cups water and add it to the meat and spices. Cook 15 minutes. Add chopped Swiss chard and simmer, covered, over low heat for 3 hours. Meanwhile, mix ground beef with coriander, mint, garlic, salt, and pepper in a large bowl. Shape mixture into 1-inch meatballs. Add meatballs and white beans to the stew, and cook, covered, over low heat for another 30 minutes. Serve with plain couscous or rice, a green salad, and a French baguette.

Recipe by Hasna Trabelsi

Rouz Djerbi

Djerbian-Style Rice with Lamb
Serves 6

This is a splendid dish, full of different tastes and aromas. Raoudha and her husband both have family origins in Djerba, so Rouz Djerbi is one of their favorite meals. When Raoudha was a young bride, she used to make huge batches to last an entire week. She served it so often that, alas, her husband pleaded with her not to prepare it anymore. Be sure to rinse and pat dry the herbs before mincing.

Ingredients

- ½ pound boneless shoulder or leg of lamb, fat removed, cut into 2-inch cubes.
- ½ tablespoon ground turmeric
- 2 tablespoons paprika
- 1 tablespoon ground coriander
- 1 cup finely chopped scallions, white and green parts
- ½ tablespoon tomato paste
- ¼ cup extra virgin olive oil
- 1 pound fresh spinach, finely chopped
- 4 cups minced fresh flat-leaf parsley leaves
- 1 tablespoon minced fresh dill leaves
- 1 cup rice

Note

You can substitute shrimp or squid, cut into long strips, for the lamb. You can also use a mixture of both shrimp and squid. Replace the coriander with cumin, and add 4 cloves garlic, peeled, minced or crushed with a garlic press.

Preparation

Place lamb, turmeric, paprika, coriander, scallions, tomato paste, oil, spinach, parsley, dill, and rice in a large bowl. Using your hands, mix together well. It's important that the spices and herbs are well combined with the rice and lamb. Place in top part of *couscousière* or steamer. Bring 12 cups water to a boil in lower part of *couscousière*. Steam, uncovered, for 40 minutes. This dish makes a great leftover meal, lasting in the refrigerator for one or two days. It freezes well.

Marka - Tunisian Stew

This vegtable-based stew is similar to the tagine served in Morocco, except it isn't cooked in a terra-cotta Moroccan bowl. Vegtables along with chicken, lamb, beef, or fish are cooked in a casserole on top of the stove. The vegetables are added toward the end, depending on how well cooked you like them. There are many different variations of *marka*. One of Raoudha's favorites is *Market Jelbena*.

Market Jelbena
Pea and Artichoke Stew with Lamb
Serves 6

Traditionally, stews in Tunisia are prepared with lamb. Today, many Tunisians substitute chicken for lamb. Both are excellent. For a less spicy flavor, replace the Anaheim peppers with Cubanell peppers or one seeded and sliced bell pepper.

Ingredients

- ½ teaspoon salt
- ¼ teaspoon freshly ground black pepper
- 1½ pounds bone-in shoulder or leg of lamb, cut in 6 pieces, or 6 chicken thighs or breasts.
- ¼ cup extra virgin olive oil
- 1 small white onion, peeled and thinly sliced
- 1 (29-ounce) can diced tomatoes, with juice
- 1 tablespoon paprika
- 2 teaspoons ground turmeric
- 2 Anaheim peppers, stems and seeds removed, quartered
- 6 fresh artichoke hearts or 12 frozen artichoke hearts
- 6 cups fresh or frozen sweet peas
- ¼ cup minced fresh flat-leaf parsley leaves

Preparation

Salt and pepper lamb. In a large pot, heat oil over low heat. Add lamb and onions, and sauté for 5 minutes. Add tomatoes with the juice, paprika, and turmeric. Stir well, increase heat to medium-high, and bring to a boil. Reduce heat to medium-low. Simmer gently, covered, until meat is tender, about forty minutes. Stir occasionally. Add ¼ cup water if sauce becomes too thick. Stir in peppers. Simmer, covered, 5 minutes over medium heat. Add artichokes and peas; mix well, and simmer, covered, 5 minutes more. Mix in parsley and cook 30 more seconds.

Note

If using fresh artichokes, remove leaves and choke, keeping only the hearts. You can use other vegetables for this stew.

Judith's version with chicken, red and purple potatoes, carrots, and cremini mushrooms

Marka Zaâra fil Koucha

Potato Stew with Lamb
Serves 6

Unlike in the United States, the principle ingredients in a stew in Tunisia are vegetables. Lamb or chicken is added for flavor. If you want to substitute chicken for the lamb, use 6 bone-in chicken thighs or small chicken breasts.

Ingredients for Sauce

2	cups hot water
1	tablespoon lemon juice
4	tablespoons extra virgin olive oil
1	tablespoon ground turmeric
½	teaspoon salt
¼	teaspoon freshly ground black pepper

Ingredients for Lamb

1½	pounds bone-in shoulder or leg of lamb, cut in 6 pieces
1	tablespoon ground coriander
4	cloves garlic, peeled, minced or crushed with a garlic press
1	small white onion, peeled and sliced
2	tablespoons extra virgin olive oil
½	teaspoon salt
¼	teaspoon freshly ground black pepper
6	sprigs fresh rosemary, whole
6	sprigs fresh thyme, whole
4	medium Yukon Gold potatoes, peeled and quartered
2	Anaheim or Cubanelle peppers, stems and seeds removed, quartered
2	plum tomatoes, quartered
2	cups fresh or frozen sweet peas, optional
8	tablespoons minced fresh flat-leaf parsley, for garnish
¼	cup finely chopped scallions, white part only, for garnish
1	tablespoon lemon juice

Preparation for Sauce

Mix hot water, lemon juice, olive oil, turmeric, salt, and pepper together in a small bowl. Set aside.

Preparation of Lamb

Preheat oven to 400°F. Place lamb in a large roasting pan. Mix coriander, garlic, onions, olive oil, salt, pepper and rosemary and thyme sprigs in a bowl. Pour over lamb, making sure both sides of the meat are well covered. Add potatoes and peppers. Layer tomatoes on top. Pour prepared sauce over meat and vegetables. Bake until sauce begins to boil, about 15 minutes. Reduce oven to 350°F, and cook for 1 hour, basting every 15 minutes. Add peas during last 5 minutes, if desired. Remove and discard herb sprigs. Mix parsley, scallions, and lemon juice in a bowl; season with salt and pepper. Serve separately in a serving bowl for the table.

Note

I replaced the Yukon Gold potatoes and peas with red and purple potatoes, carrots, and cremini mushrooms. Use your imagination with the various ingredients.

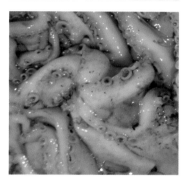

Fish

The Fish Market
at La Goulette

Since a vast majority of the population in Tunisia resides along the coast, fish is a popular dish. Tunisians buy their fish fresh, ideally caught the same day. It's usually grilled whole on an outdoor barbecue over wood charcoal.

When I was a Peace Corps Volunteer, we used to take a 15-minute train ride to the seaside port of La Goulette. Here we bought our fish, usually *daurade* (sea bream) or *loup* (branzino), from a fishmonger. We then took it to one of the many sidewalk cafés to have it grilled on a wood charcoal barbecue and ate it accompanied by a Tunisian white wine.

The Fish Market
at La Goulette

The memory of those cool summer evenings by the sea, feasting on grilled fresh fish with the lingering taste of cumin and lemon, remains with me fifty years later. Raoudha and Hasna go to the same fish market in La Goulette that we went to so many years ago. They insist it's one of the best in the area. In the past, before air-conditioning, many inhabitants of Tunis would move to La Goulette for the summer season.

Hout Mechoui

Grilled Fish
Serves 4

Ingredients

4 medium whole fish,
    scaled and cleaned
    Extra virgin olive oil
½ teaspoon salt
2 teaspoons cumin
    Lemon wedges

Mixing cumin with salt

Tunisians like to grill their fish seasoned with cumin, salt, and pepper. This simple recipe is delicious and easy to do on the barbecue. Tunisians adore cooking fish, especially grilling it. We suggest the following fish: *daurade* (sea bream), *loup* (branzino), red snapper, or sardines.

Preparation

Heat grill to medium. Make three or four ¼-inch deep diagonal slits across one side of the fish. Brush fish with some olive oil, so it won't stick to the grill. Finally, season the fish with salt and cumin. A medium fish requires 5 to 7 minutes grilling on each side over medium heat. Garnish with a lemon wedge. Serve with a green salad, *Slata Mechouïa*, page 29, *Kafteji*, page 109, or *Tastira*, page 111.

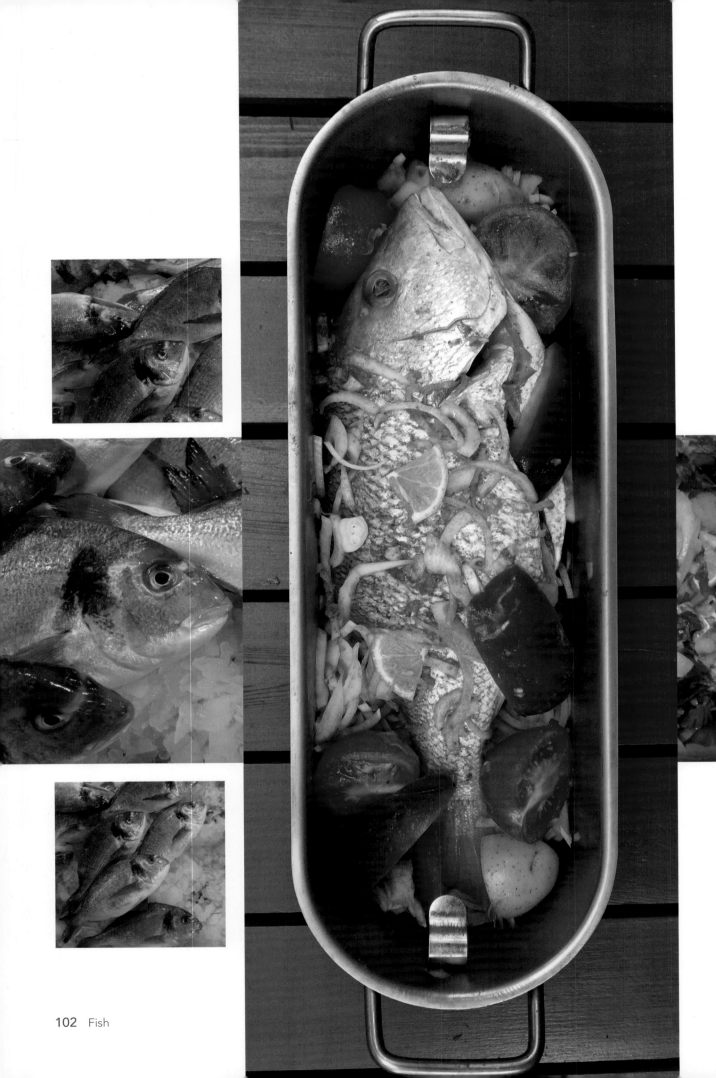

Ingredients for Fish

- 2 to 3 pounds fish, scaled and cleaned, left whole or cut into 6 serving pieces
- 4 cloves garlic, peeled, minced or crushed with a garlic press
- 3 tablespoons ground cumin
- 1 tablespoon ground turmeric
- ½ teaspoon salt
- ¼ teaspoon freshly ground black pepper
- 4 small Yukon Gold potatoes, peeled and quartered
- 2 plum tomatoes, quartered
- 2 Anaheim or Cubanelle peppers, stems and seeds removed, quartered
- 1 large white onion, peeled and thinly sliced
- 2 slices lemon, cut into small pieces

Hout fel Koucha
Baked Fish
Serves 6

Serving your guests a whole baked fish surrounded by colorful red and green vegetables is always impressive and a great festive dish for any dinner party. At the fish market, choose a large fish like red snapper, branzino, or sea bream. When baking, either cut the fish into serving pieces or leave it whole. Seasoning the fish with cumin and turmeric gives it an orange hue. For more color, you can substitute small red or purple potatoes for the Yukon Gold potatoes.

Preparation

Preheat oven to 350°F. If baking the fish whole, cut 4 diagonal slits, ¼ inch deep, into one side of fish. In a small bowl, mix together garlic, cumin, turmeric, salt, and pepper; rub on fish.

Ingredients for Sauce

- 4 cloves garlic, peeled, minced or crushed with a garlic press
- 2 tablespoons ground cumin
- 1 tablespoon ground turmeric
- 2 tablespoons extra virgin olive oil
- ½ teaspoon salt
- ¼ teaspoon freshly ground black pepper
  Minced fresh flat-leaf parsley leaves for garnish
  Scallions, white and green parts, finely chopped for garnish

Place potatoes in a large rimmed baking pan or fish poacher, and place fish on top. Arrange tomatoes, peppers, and onions around the fish, and lemons on top. In a small bowl, make a sauce with garlic, cumin, turmeric, olive oil, salt, pepper, and 2 cups water; mix well. Pour sauce over fish. Bake 30 minutes, basting a few times with the sauce. Cover baking pan with a lid or tin foil, and bake until fish and potatoes are done, 20 to 25 minutes more. Test with a fork: the fish should flake easily and potatoes should be tender. Before serving, garnish fish and vegetables with parsley and scallions.

Hout Mokli

Fried Fish
Serves 4

If you can't find tiny fish for frying, buy fresh sardines and you can either fry them or grill them on top of the stove on a grill pan. Either way, fried or grilled, this is a tasty and inexpensive meal. Most Tunisians eat the entire small fish, head and tail included.

Ingredients

1 tablespoon ground cumin
½ teaspoon salt
16 tiny fish like smelts
   or red mullets or 4 sardines
   scaled and cleaned
1 tablespoon all-purposed
   flour
3 tablespoons vegetable oil
   Lemon wedges for garnish

Preparation

Rub cumin and salt over the fish. Pour flour in a shallow plate, and dip the whole fish in the flour. Heat oil in a large frying pan over medium-high heat until oil is shimmering. Add fish, and fry for 3 minutes on each side. Fry sardines, for 4 minutes on each side.

Note

If using sardines, you can also use a grill pan on top of the stove. Rub fish with salt and cumin, and make diagonal slits across the fish. You don't need to dip the sardines in flour. Add a small amount of olive oil to the grill pan, and grill 4 minutes on each side over medium heat. Serve hot.

Ingredients for Stuffing

4   large or 8 small squid, cleaned, bodies and tentacles separated

¼   cup minced fresh flat-leaf parsley leaves

½   cup minced scallions, white and green parts

1   tablespoon minced fresh dill leaves

1   tablespoon rice, rinsed and drained

4   cloves garlic, peeled, minced or crushed with a garlic press

½   teaspoon tomato paste

1   teaspoon paprika

½   teaspoon ground turmeric

1   teaspoon ground cumin

½   teaspoon salt

¼   teaspoon freshly ground black pepper

Ingredients for Tomato Sauce

5   tablespoons extra virgin olive oil

5   cloves garlic, peeled, minced or crushed with a garlic press

1   teaspoon ground cumin

1   medium onion, peeled and *chopped*

1   teaspoon paprika

1   (28 ounce) can imported Italian plum tomatoes, with juice, diced

½   teaspoon ground turmeric

2   to 3 cups warm water

½   teaspoon salt

¼   teaspoon freshly ground black pepper

Calamars Farcis
Stuffed Calamari (Squid)
Serves 4

The secret to this recipe is to buy the squid already cleaned. It isn't difficult to find squid at any good supermarket purveying fresh fish. The stuffed calamari is slowly simmered in a tomato sauce in a large pan on top of the stove. This is not a common dish in America, but I found it easy to prepare, and inexpensive. Be sure to cook the squid over very low heat since its flesh is dense and can become rubbery if cooked too quickly.

Squid pockets and
its tentacles

Preparation for Stuffing

Rinse out squid pockets or sacs under cold water, and pat thoroughly dry with a cloth or paper towels. Mince the tentacles. Place the tentacles, parsley, scallions, dill, rice, garlic, tomato paste, paprika, turmeric, cumin, salt, and pepper in a bowl, and mix well. Stuff each squid body pocket only two-thirds full with this mixture. Secure with a toothpick. Be sure not to overstuff the pockets or they might burst in cooking. Prick the skin with a toothpick in several places. Set aside while preparing the tomato sauce.

Preparation Tomato Sauce

Heat olive oil in a large frying pan over low heat. Add garlic, and sauté until you smell its aroma. Add cumin, and stir in for a few seconds. Add onions and sauté until onions are translucent, about 3 minutes. Add garlic and sauté another 30 to 60 seconds. Stir in paprika, and then tomatoes with their juice. Reduce heat to low. Cover, and cook at a very slow simmer until most of the liquid has evaporated, about 15 minutes. Add turmeric, the stuffed squid, and enough warm water to completely cover the squid. Bring back to a simmer and cook, stirring occasionally and turning squid several times while basting, over low heat for 45 to 60 minutes, depending on the size and thickness of the squid. The squid is done if it feels tender when gently prodded with a fork. Remove from heat. Season with salt and pepper. Arrange the stuffed calamari on a platter, and pour tomato sauce over top. Serve with couscous or rice.

Note

You can also serve this dish with the vegetables and eggs left whole, as illustrated. When prepared in this manner, the Tunisians call it *Shan Mokli*.

Ingredients

Vegetable oil

4   small new potatoes, peeled and cut as French fries

2   zucchini, rinsed, sliced into 2½ inch rounds

½   pound butternut or acorn squash, peeled, seeded and sliced into 1 inch pieces

4   tomatoes, halved

4   Anaheim peppers, left whole

2   large eggs

1   teaspoon dried mint, finely crushed

1   teaspoon ground coriander

½   teaspoon salt

¼   teaspoon freshly ground black pepper

Vegetables and eggs served whole, called *Shan Mokli*

Kafteji
Fried Vegetables
Serves 6

This dish usually accompanies grilled fish. It can also be a light meal in itself. Raoudha's son, Wajih, says this is one of his favorite meals. It's an extremely popular dish in Tunisia. You can make it as spicy as you like by choosing mild Cubanelle peppers, slightly spicy Anaheim, or New Mexico peppers that have more of a kick to them. To prepare, plan on a good 45 minutes.

Tunisian green peppers

Preparation

Line a baking sheet with paper towels. Heat 3 tablespoons oil in a large frying pan over medium-high heat. Fry all vegetables separately. Start with the potatoes. Fry, turning occasionally, until tender, about 10 minutes. Transfer to paper towels to drain. Add and heat more vegetable oil to frying pan as each vegetable is fried, if needed. Fry zucchini for 3 minutes. Transfer to the paper towels. Fry butternut squash for 4 minutes. Transfer to paper towels. Fry tomatoes for 3 minutes. Transfer to paper towels. Fry peppers whole until the skin is charred. Transfer and let cool on paper towels or in a clean paper bag for 15 minutes. Trapping the moist heat helps to loosen the skin. Use a small knife or your fingers to peel off the skins.

When cooled, skin, seed, and remove stems of peppers and tomatoes. Chop all vegetables into small pieces and put them in a bowl. Heat 3 tablespoons oil in a small frying pan, and fry the eggs. Chop up fried eggs and mix with the vegetables. Sit in mint, coriander, salt, and pepper.

Tastira
Fried Peppers and Tomatoes
Serves 6

Tunisians often serve this classic recipe as a side dish to accompany grilled or fried fish. Normally served chopped, the vegetables can also be left whole as illustrated.

Chopped tomatoes
and peppers

Grilled fish below served
with green peppers and
French fried potatoes

Sliced fried
peppers,
tomatoes,
and eggs

Ingredients

3 tablespoons vegetable oil
4 Anaheim or Cubanelle peppers, left whole
6 plum tomatoes, halved lengthwise
1 teaspoon ground coriander
2 cloves garlic, peeled, minced or crushed with a garlic press
½ teaspoon salt
¼ teaspoon freshly ground black pepper
1 large egg, optional

Preparation

In a large frying pan, heat vegetable oil over medium heat, and fry peppers until charred. Remove peppers and set aside on paper towels or in a clean paper bag. Fry tomatoes in the same pan until charred. Add and heat more oil if necessary. Transfer to paper towels to drain and cool down. When cooled, skin, seed, and remove stems and seeds of peppers and tomatoes. Dice tomatoes and peppers, and put the vegetables in a bowl. Add coriander, garlic, salt, and pepper; mix well. If you wish, fry an egg, chop it up, and mix in with rest of ingredients.

Desserts

Fruit

Most Tunisians prefer a simple dessert of fresh fruit and dates. Picked seasonally, the extraordinary variety of fruits is exceptional and abundant, be they melons, grapes, strawberries, sun-dried dates, apples, pomegranates, pears, or oranges. Nothing is more refreshing than a bowl of fresh fruit seasoned with orange or rose blossom water.

Prickly Pears in Dougga
Ancient Roman City

September is the season for prickly pears, large pear-shaped fruits that grow on cactus plants. Tunisians like to cut them open and devour them right from the farmers' fruit stand. At the ancient Roman archeological site, Dougga, we found wonderful examples of the cactus plants in full bloom.

Dougga

Green olives

Fruit and Vegetable Stand

On our way home from our visit to the magnificent Roman city of Dougga, we noticed a fruit and vegetable stand in Testour. Our hosts insisted we stop, taste, and fill their trunk with fresh fruit.

Along the side of the roads, farmers sell fresh fruit, vegetables, and olives right off their trucks or in covered stands located next to their orchards. In the fall, the farmers' stands overflow with boxes of pomegranates, pears, green olives, and apples.

Mint Tea and Pastries

After dinner, the Tunisian tradition calls for people to leave the dining room table and congregate in another room for digestive mint tea and pastries. This ritual gives everyone a chance to relax and continue the conversation in new surroundings. Raoudha prides herself on pouring tea the Tunisian way, holding the teapot high above the glass to aerate the tea. On special occasions, many people add pine nuts to their glass of tea.

Mint tea with
pine nuts

Hasna

Pastries

Today most Tunisians buy their pastries at a bakery or pastry shop where they can pick from a wide assortment of Tunisian, Middle Eastern, and French pastries.

Some Tunisian women, however, still prepare their own pastries. *Samsa* and *Makroudh* are two of Hasna's and Raoudha's favorite homemade desserts.

Roasted Hazelnuts

Grinding nuts

Dipping in syrup

Samsa
Crushed Nut-Filled Pastry
Makes approximately 36 pastries

I found this recipe surprisingly easy to prepare. I substituted Greek phyllo dough sheets for *malsouka brik* dough sheets. For this recipe, Raoudha prefers a mixture of almonds and hazelnuts, even though the traditional Tunisian recipe is based on ground sesame seeds.

Ingredients

2   tablespoons granulated sugar
1   cup coarsely ground almonds, hazelnuts, sesame seeds, or pistachios
3   tablespoons orange or rose blossom water
3   *sheets brik (malsouka)* or 9 sheets Greek phyllo
2   tablespoons butter, melted

Ingredients for Syrup

2   cups granulated sugar
1½ teaspoons fresh lemon juice
1½ teaspoons rose or orange blossom water

Preparation

Combine sugar, nuts, and blossom water in a bowl. Preheat oven to 350°F. Cut the sheets of dough into 2-inch wide crosswise strips. Using a pastry brush, lightly brush each strip with melted butter. Place 1 teaspoon nut mixture at the top of each strip. Fold each strip back and forth on the diagonal from top to bottom of the strip. See illustration. Be sure the nut mixture doesn't fall out of the resulting triangular pocket.

Place the triangles on a rimmed baking sheet. Bake until golden brown and crispy, about 10 minutes on each side. In the meantime, prepare the syrup. Combine the sugar and 1 cup water in a pot, and simmer over low heat, stirring until the sugar and water are well mixed, and sugar is dissolved. Bring to a boil, and stir in the lemon juice. Be careful mixture doesn't burn. When the mixture turns golden brown, add blossom water. Cook 30 more seconds. Remove from heat. Test syrup by putting a few drops of syrup on a plate and letting it cool. The texture must be like thick honey. If it's too thick, add 1 or 2 tablespoons of blossom water. If it's too liquid, boil the syrup another 2 or 3 minutes.

When the pastry triangles are down, remove from the oven. Immediately drop the hot triangles, a few at a time, with a slotted spoon into the hot syrup for a few seconds to coat the pastry. Drain the excess syrup off the pastry triangles, and place on a serving dish. Let cool. These are best eaten cold. You can even serve them the next day. Since I prefer a less sweet pastry, I skip the final step of dipping them into the syrup.

Ingredients for Date Pastry

3 cups semolina
1 cup all-purpose flour
1 cup warm extra virgin olive oil
1 cup warm water
½ teaspoon salt
½ teaspoon baking soda
2 cups sliced pitted dates
1 tablespoon ground cinnamon
¼ cup extra virgin olive oil
  Vegetable oil
  Sesame seeds, (optional)

Ingredients for Syrup

2 cups granulated sugar
½ tablespoon fresh lemon juice
½ tablespoon rose or
  orange blossom water

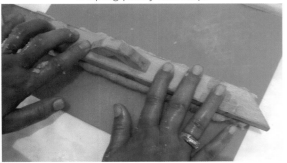
Shaping pastry into strips

Using wooden press, *tabâa makroudh*

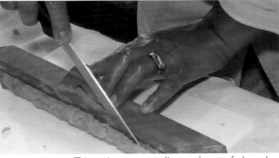
Placing crushed dates in depression

Trimming protruding edges of dough

Cutting pastry on the diagonal

Makroudh
Date Pastry
Makes approximately 30 date pastries

This dessert takes some practice to make. When I tried making it for the first time, it didn't come close to the lovely looking date pastries made by Raoudha and Hasna. Nevertheless, they tasted good. Be courageous. Practice makes perfect.

Preparation of Date Pastry and Syrup

Mix semolina and flour together in a bowl. Add warm olive oil, and mix well with your hands. In another bowl, mix warm water with salt and baking soda. Add to flour mixture, and delicately mix until dough has completely absorbed the water. Let dough sit for 30 minutes. In the meantime, place dates, cinnamon, and another ¼ cup olive oil in a food processor; pulse to form a paste. Divide the dough into three equal pieces. Using your hands, shape the dough into strips, 1½ inches wide and 12 inches long. With the side of your hand, create a deep depression along the length of each strip. See illustration. Fill this depression with the date paste, and pinch it together with your thumb and forefinger. Flatten dough with your hands or a special Tunisian wooden press called a *tabâa makroudh*. See illustration. With a knife, trim excess dough on each side so that the sides of the strips are straight and even. See illustration. Cut on the diagonal into approximately 1-inch pieces. See illustration. Set aside.

Prepare the syrup. Combine sugar and 1 cup water in a pot, and simmer over low heat, stirring, until well mixed and sugar is dissolved. Bring to a boil, and stir in lemon juice. When mixture turns golden brown, add some blossom water. Be careful mixture doesn't burn. Cook 30 more seconds. Remove from heat. Test syrup by putting a few drops of syrup on a plate and letting it cool. The texture must be like thick honey. If it's too thick, add 1 or 2 tablespoons of blossom water. If it's too liquid, boil the syrup another 2 or 3 minutes. Set aside to cool.

In a deep frying pan, heat about 1-inch vegetable oil over medium-low heat. Using a slotted spoon, place pastries in oil, and fry until golden on both sides. Be careful, if oil gets too hot, the pastries could burn. Remove and dip immediately into the cooled syrup for a few seconds. Drain in a strainer and let cool on paper towels. You can sprinkle sesame seeds on top if desired.

Crima
Tunisian Custard
Serves 6

When Tunisians do serve a homemade dessert, they often prepare *crima*, a custard similar to, but thicker than, *crème anglaise*. During the Islamic month of Ramadan, *crima* is often served late at night after *Iftar*, the festive breaking-of-the-fast meal.

Preparation

Place cornstarch in a bowl. Add ¼-cup milk, and stir to dissolve. Stir in the rest of the milk. In a separate bowl, beat egg yolks well with sugar until it forms a ribbon. Add vanilla bean, orange blossom water, and milk mixture to eggs. Pour into a 4-quart pot. Stir continually over medium-low heat until mixture thickens enough to coat the back of a spoon. Remove from heat. Remove and discard vanilla bean. Put crumbled cookies in small serving bowls or glasses. Pour custard on top. Sprinkle almonds or pistachio nuts on top of the custard. Serve at room temperature, or, even better, cold.

Ingredients

- 3 tablespoons cornstarch
- 4 cups whole milk
- 4 large egg yolks
- 3 tablespoons sugar
- 1 vanilla bean
- ¼ cup orange blossom water
- 3 to 4 oatmeal, date, walnut or almond cookies, crumbled
- 1 tablespoon chopped almonds
- 1 tablespoon chopped pistachio nuts

Pomegranate arils

Masfouf
Sweet Couscous
Serves 6 to 8

With this dessert, you can be as inventive as you want, adding to the sweet couscous any combination of nuts, dates, pomegranates, grapes, or raisins. It depends on what you have in your kitchen at the time. Tunisians generally have this dessert during the month of Ramadan. They serve it just before dawn to mark the beginning of the next daylong fast. If you don't have time to prepare the traditional couscous from scratch, buy a commercial packaged fine grain couscous and follow the instructions on the box.

Ingredients

1 cup fine grain couscous
2 tablespoons extra virgin olive oil
½ cup sugar
2 tablespoons butter
¼ cup orange blossom or rose water
2 cups total fresh pomegranate arils and seedless grapes or
2 cups total chopped dates, raisins, and/or sun-dried cranberries, or
2 cups total chopped walnuts, almonds, pistachios, and/or pine nuts

Preparation

Pour the couscous in a bowl. Add olive oil and mix well. Add 3/4 cup water, a few drops at a time, mixing well with your hands so that all the grains are evenly moistened. Let stand for 10 minutes so the grains absorb the water and expand, thus keeping the grains from falling through the holes in the *couscousière* or steamer. Skip this entire process if using a commercial packaged fine grain couscous. Bring 6 cups water to boil in bottom part of *couscousière*. Put the couscous in the top part of a *couscousière* or steamer over the boiling water and cover with lid. The moment the steam begins to penetrate the couscous grains, continue cooking for 30 more minutes over medium heat. If the grains are still hard and crunchy, continue steaming them for another 10 to 15 minutes. Remove the couscous and put it in a serving bowl. Break up any lumps before serving. Stir the sugar into the couscous, then stir in the butter, and then the blossom water.

Stir in 2 cups of mixed fruits and nuts of your choice. You can also arrange some of the fruit as decoration on top. See illustration. It's up to you, use your imagination.

Spices and Herbs

It's always a pleasure to wander through the spice stalls, filled with vibrant colors and tantalizing aromas. in any neighborhood or souk (market place) of a Tunisian town. Vendors artfully display their spices in large bins for all to admire. The most common spices used in Tunisian cuisine are turmeric, cumin, coriander, paprika, cinnamon, salt, and black pepper. Garlic is also an added ingredient in many dishes.

Turmeric

Known as *curcum* in Arabic, this vibrant yellow orange spice is made from the ground dried roots of the *Curcuma longa* plant, native to India. Turmeric has an earthy, slightly peppery, mustard-like flavor. In India and Southeast Asia, this plant has been used for thousands of years as both a dye and as a medicine. Recent laboratory and animal research studies show that turmeric has an array of potentially beneficial properties from treating or preventing arthritis, inflammation, indigestion, and colitis to treating cancer, cardiovascular disease, dementia, depression, diabetes, skin diseases, and ulcers. It's clear why so many people are calling turmeric the miracle spice.

Cumin

Cumin has been a favorite Tunisian spice since ancient times. It's made from the seeds of the herb, *Cuminun cyminum*, a member of the parsley family. It has a sweet, earthy, smoky taste. Like turmeric, it also has health benefits. Many people claim it's especially good when you have indigestion or a stomachache.

Herbs

Parsley, mint, dill, rosemary, basil, oregano, thyme, and bay leaves are the most popular herbs used in Tunisian cooking.

Rose Blossom

Orange Blossom

131

Harissa

Tunisians love their *harissa*, especially if it's homemade. *Harissa* adds a spicy kick to many dishes. Connoisseurs even like to spread it on fresh bread. Raoudha insists that *harissa* isn't hard to prepare as long as you can find dried red chili peppers. When you make homemade *harissa*, the flavors are fresher and the color more vibrant than with the store- bought variety.

An ancient Tunisian legend recounts how a husband would judge his wife's affections by the amount of hot peppers she used when preparing the *harissa*. If it wasn't spicy enough, it was a sign that she no longer loved him.

Note

You need to have an airtight sterilzed glass container for this recipe.

Avoid touching your eyes when handling the dried red chili peppers.

Ingredients

1 pound dried red chili peppers, stems and seeds removed. Boiling water
2 medium heads garlic, cloves separated and peeled
2 tablespoons salt
2 tablespoons ground coriander
½ cup extra virgin olive oil, plus more if needed

Preparation

Place the dried peppers in a bowl. Add boiling water to cover, and soak for 30 minutes. Drain and dry with paper towels. Transfer the peppers to a food processer. Add garlic, and pulse until coarsely chopped. Add salt, coriander, and oil; process into a paste. Add more oil if needed. Put the *harissa* in an airtight sterilized glass container, and top it off with a little bit of olive oil to keep it from drying out. Keep refrigerated.

Limoun
Preserved Lemons

Throughout the Mediterranean region, most pantries store preserved lemons. It takes one month of curing in a water-filled jar to preserve the lemons. It's definitely worth the wait.

Ingredients

Water
1   large egg
    Salt
2   tablespoons white vinegar
    Lemons, rinsed and left whole

Preparation

Fill a Mason jar with water, and the egg. Stir in enough salt that the egg floats to the top. Remove the egg, and pour the water into a pitcher with the vinegar. Pack the Mason jar full of fresh lemons. Add the prepared vinegar and salt water. Tightly seal the jar, and let sit for at least a month. Refrigerate after opening.

Preserved lemons

Oumelleh
Pickled Vegetables

Tunisians love their pickled vegtables; pickling allows them to enjoy their favorites year round. This is a very forgiving recipe. Choose whatever vegetables you have on hand and as many as will fit into your jar. Like with the preserved lemons, the vegetables must cure in a mixture of salt, vinegar, and water for at least a month.

Ingredients

1   large egg
    Salt
    Carrots, turnips, celery, or Persian cucumber, peeled, and cut into 2-inch slices
    Green beans, fennel, or cauliflower, rinsed, and cut into 2 to 3-inch pieces
2   tablesoons white vinegar

Preparation

Fill a Mason jar with water and the egg. Stir in enough salt that the egg floats to the top. Remove the egg, and pour the water into a pot and bring to a boil. Place a combination of the vegetables that you want to preserve into a Mason jar and fill with hot salt water and the vinegar. Seal the jar and let sit for at least one month. In the refrigerator, pickled vegetables can last for a year.

Pickled vegetables

Where to Buy Tunisian Ingredients

Most ingredients can be found in the United States, at Whole Foods, Trader Joe's, Le Pain Quotidien, Zingerman's, or online at amazon.com, or at www.bobsredmill.com. You can also visit *Les Moulins Mahjoub* at www.moulinsmahjoub.com, or their importer, Rogers Collection at www.RogersCollection.us who can also direct you to local United States retailers. Most supermarkets carry the grains mentioned in this cookbook. You can find Tunisian ingredients at most Middle Eastern specialty grocery stores.

Couscous

You can buy couscous in the bins at Whole Foods, Trader Joe's, or online at Rogers Collection at www.RogersCollection.us. All supermarkets have the commercial packaged couscous. You can also buy couscous at Middle Eastern grocery stores.

M'hamsa

You can buy *M'hamsa* at Whole Foods and Le Pain Quotidien under the label of Rogers Collection or online at amazon.com, or www.RogersCollection.us. If unavailable, substitute the commercial packaged Israeli couscous.

Harissa

Harissa can be found at Whole Foods, Trader Joe's, and Le Pain Quotidien. You can also find it online at amazon.com, Rogers Collection at www.RogersCollection.us.

Freekeh

You can buy *freekeh* at most upscale grocery stores, Middle Eastern shops, organic food stores, online at Rogers Collection at www.RogersCollection.us, or amazon.com under Bob's Red Mill Organic Whole Grain Cracked Freekeh.

Brik

You can order sheets of *brik* dough (*malsouka*) online from levillage.com or amazon.com under *Brik* Dough – *Feuilles de Brik*. You can also buy it in Middle Eastern grocery stores under the names *malsouka* or *feuilles de brik*.

Couscousière or Couscous Pot

You can find the couscous pot on amazon.com or in most specialty cooking stores. You can also use a steamer, or a regular stockpot with a vegetable steamer. If the holes are too big, line the steamer with a piece of cheesecloth, so the couscous grains won't fall through the holes.

Couscous

M'hamsa

Harissa

Sheet of folded brik

Couscousière

Vendor selling bread in Nabeul

Acknowledgments

We wish to thank all our friends who enthusiastically tested different recipes in our cookbook to make sure they worked for American cooks.

Sharon Blinko
Susan Borke
Audrey Brunetaux
Lewis and Monique Cohen
Maggie Eads
Andrea Foster
Phylis Geller
Ruth Gramlich
Jong Soo Hallet
Marian Johnson
Betty Kotcher
Jennifer Lawson
Susan Lerner
Liz Magnes
Conn Martin
Gail Massot
Tracy Orloff
Suzanne Owen
Melita Westerlund
Donna Wolverton

Text and recipes edited with great care by:

Paula Jacobson
Sheilah Kaufman

Offset printing patiently overseen by :

Sreed Vijayarangam
Assistant to the President
Insight Editions, LP

We could never have written this cookbook without the support of Raoudha's husband, Khaldoun Ben Taarit, who enthusiastically encouraged us to take on the project. Thank you to Abdesselem Trabelsi, Hasna's husband, who drove us back and forth between Raoudha's kitchen and the kitchen in our small hotel, Dar Marsa Cubes, where the staff was so supportive. A big thank you goes to the late Moncef Meddeb, a celebrated Tunisian chef who made a name for himself in the United States before retiring to Tunisia. He received the prestigious James Beard Award in 1986. He patiently went over every recipe, informing me, "Judy, there's a special language for cookbooks!" We also thank our tasters who joined us at the dinner table in Tunisia: Ramsi and Virginie Gallali and their three daughters, George and Conn Martin, Richard Loosle, Robert Hermanson, Travis Price, and Ryan Novi. A special thanks to Cindy Nguyen and her husband, Matt Hall, "Mr. Lumière," for helping me set up the lights and tripod to photograph several of the dishes during their stay in Tunisia. An extra special thank you to our son, Jong Soo, who also gave his invaluable feedback about many of the recipes in Tunisia as well as those that he tested in America.

In the United States, we invited many friends to taste the different and, to them, exotic meals: Roger and Ellen Lewis, Katie and Gerard Huet, Suzanne and Jim Owen, Steve and Susan Katona, Judith Goldstein, Fabienne Lips-Dumas and Tim Fritzpatrick, Monique and Lewis Cohen, Trish and Jason Williams, Alison Richards and Ron Dreben, Liz and Rafi Magnes, Allan Gerson, Allison Argo, Edward and AJ Friedman, Aviva Kempner, Pamela Drexel, and Mary Kirk. Thank you to Susan Barocas for her invaluable input. A special thank you for the advice and support from our friend, the renowned cookbook author, Joan Nathan, and for her suggestion to take American measuring cups and spoons to Tunisia. Thank you to Phil Jones, Ken Crerar of Rogers Collection and Majib and Abdelwaheb Mahjoub who generously gave us permission to include several photographs of their lovely farm. A thank you to Paula Jacobson and Sheilah Kaufman for their enthusiastic support and extraordinary editing of our text. And to Stéphanie Cardot for one more final proofreading.

Author Biographies

Judith Dwan Hallet

Judith is an award-winning documentary filmmaker who has been making films for nearly 50 years. After graduating from college in 1964, she joined the Peace Corps in Tunisia teaching English as a foreign language (TEFL). She also made a film on the Berber Villages of Southern Tunisia with her now husband, architect/filmmaker Stanley Hallet. After directing several more independent films with Stanley, including two documentaries in Afghanistan, Judith became a Producer/Reporter at KUTV, the NBC affiliate in Salt Lake City, Utah. Moving to Washington, D.C. in 1986, Judith was hired by National Geographic Television to be the Senior Producer for EXPLORER, their weekly television series. While at the helm, she produced and directed four films including a documentary on Jane Goodall. In 1991, Judy formed her own company, Judith Dwan Hallet Productions. Over her career, Judith has produced films in 17 countries on subjects as diverse as an obscure tribe living in tree houses in the rainforest of Papua on the Island of New Guinea, the gauchos in Argentina, Pope John Paul II, and the return of the buffalo to American Indian reservations.

Judith earned a BA from Sarah Lawrence College and an MA in French from the University of Utah following graduate studies at the School of Motion Pictures at UCLA.

Judith and Stanley Hallet live in Washington, D.C., in a house that Stanley designed. Their son, Jong Soo Hallet, is Co-Founder & VP of Marketing at Paylitix, a tech startup headquartered in Utah. Writing a cookbook on Tunisian cuisine was a natural transition for someone who loves to document different cultures and taste tantalizing cuisines. This is her first cookbook. She has also written *Adventures of a Documentary Filmmaker*, a behind-the-scenes memoir on her professional life of making films around the world.

Dedicated to:

the loving memories of our mothers, Lois Smith Dwan, Wassila Ouerghi Guellali, and Habiba Trabelsi, for their endless kindness and devotion, and for introducing us to the love of food and the art of cooking.

Raoudha Guellali Ben Taarit

Raoudha grew up on the banks of the Medjerda River in Northern Tunisia. Her mother's ancestors came from Andalusia in the early 16th century and her father's family dates back thousands of years to a Berber village on the Island of Djerba in Southern Tunisia. Raoudha learned to prepare both Berber and Andalusian traditional dishes from these two distinct cultures. In Tunisia, recipes have always been passed down from mother to daughter and from mother-in-law to daughter-in-law. This was how Raoudha learned to cook.

Raoudha married and moved to France in her early twenties where she pursued an engineering degree at the University of Paris VI. While in France, she also developed her love for French food. She experimented with the two different cuisines, fusing Tunisian recipes with French ones.

An avid traveler, Raoudha wants to expose Tunisian cuisine to other cultures. For her, taste breaks national barriers. In 2015, Raoudha decided to take on a new challenge and write a cookbook on Tunisian cuisine with her American friend, Judith Hallet, on Tunisian cuisine with the goal of mainstreaming this rich and healthful Mediterranean diet to an international audience. Raoudha wishes to introduce Americans to Tunisian dishes that are simple yet elegant, dishes that never fail to let the essence of the fresh ingredients—herbs, spices, and bright colors—shine through. Raoudha and her husband, Khaldoun Ben Taarit, the President of l'Université Tunis Carthage live in Carthage, Tunisia, while their son, Wajih, works in Los Angeles, California.

Hasna Trabelsi

Hasna grew up in M'hamedia, a small village outside of Tunis. She married young and moved with her husband, Abdesselem Trabelsi, to Carthage. She began working as a cook for several foreign diplomat families in Tunis. Many of the embassies also hired her to cook for their diplomatic receptions. Over the years, she introduced many traditional Tunisian dishes to her foreign employers and their guests. Eventually she worked as chef for the Canadian, Italian, and French embassies, where she continued to perfect and experiment with different regional Tunisian dishes.

Today Hasna cooks for Raoudha and Khaldoun Ben Taarit. She and her husband have four children, Dorsaf, Dora, Hamza, and Donia. The three oldest have all graduated with culinary art diplomas, carrying on their mother's love of cooking. The fourth daughter is in high school.

Fishing boats on the island of Djerba

Index

Index

Index

View of the water from the Fort of Hammamet

Discovering Tunisian Cuisine
Judith Dwan Hallet
Raoudha Guellali Ben Taarit
Hasna Trabelsi

Photography Copyright © 2019
by Judith Dwan Hallet and Stanley Ira Hallet
unless otherwise credited.

Graphic Design by Stanley Ira Hallet
Indesign Software and Avenir font

All recipes are credited to
Raoudha Guellali Ben Taarit
unless otherwise noted.

Publishers:
Spirit of Place/Spirit of Design, Inc
Washington, DC, USA
http://www.spiritofplace-design.com

ISBN Number: 978-1-7923-1830-6

Keywords:
1. Discovering Tunisian Cuisine.
2. Tunisian Cookbooks. 3.Tunisian Cuisine.
4. Tunisia. 5. Djerba. 6. Tunis.
7. North African Cuisine.
8. Mediterranean Cuisine.
9. Cookbooks

Printed in China
under the supervision of
Raoul Goff
CEO of Insight Editions

First Edition 2019

Graphic design by Stanley Ira Hallet
Indesign software and Avenir font

Sunset in Southern Tunisia